Storytelling in Preaching

Storytelling in PREACHING

A Guide to the Theory and Practice

Bruce C. Salmon

BROADMAN PRESS
Nashville, Tennessee

Unless otherwise stated, all Scripture references are from the Revised Standard
Version of the Bible, copyrighted 1946, 1952, © 1971, 1973.
Scripture references marked NIV are from HOLY BIBLE, *New International
Version*, copyright © 1978, New York Bible Society. Used by permission.

Library of Congress Cataloging-in-Publication Data

Salmon, Bruce C., 1951-
Storytelling in preaching.

Bibliography: p.
1. Preaching.   2. Storytelling—Religious aspects—
Christianity.   I. Title.
BV4235.S76S25   1988   251'.08   87-26810
ISBN 0-8054-2118-1 (pbk.)

Contents

Preface

The trouble with most books on preaching is that they are written by good preachers. By that I mean they are written by extraordinarily gifted preachers. You've heard them—persons endowed with eloquence, wit, charm, perception, intellect, dramatic flair, a deep resonant voice, commanding pulpit presence, charisma. The trouble is, when we try to copy their methods, we come across as cheap imitations. This book is different. Its author is not an outstanding preacher; at best, he is a shade above ordinary. He knows what it is like to struggle with a sermon. I do it every week.

My style is not the "Saturday Night Special." I cannot generate an entire sermon in the wee hours of the night before Sunday. Neither do I have the "gift of gab." I cannot extemporaneously deliver a worthy sermon from a few scribbled notes. To preach a decent sermon, I need all the preparation I can muster. Thus, I generally spend the entire week, off and on, preparing my Sunday morning message.

It usually begins on Sunday night, often with a tinge of disappointment about the morning's effort and a resolve to do better next time. The disappointment turns into anxiety on Monday and Tuesday as a text is selected, exegeted, thought and wrought over. Occasionally there are restless nights as the chaotic movement of sermon ideas inside my head seeks expression. Wednesday and Thursday are the days of creative crisis when thoughts are applied to paper. By Friday the sermon is sometimes written, more often half written, but still it does not satisfy. Revisions continue into Saturday night. Sunday comes, and whether the sermon is ready or not, it must be born.

This is a book for persons for whom preaching does not come easily. It is a book for beginning preachers and for more experienced preachers who are looking for ways to do better. It is a book for people who agonize over sermons, who wrestle with sermon fragments in their sleep. It is a book for preachers who fail at preaching more often than they care to remember, but who somehow find the resolve to try again.

It is precisely because I am not a naturally gifted preacher that this book may be helpful. When baseball Hall of Famer Ted Williams became the manager of the Washington Senators, sports writers and fans immediately began to look for the team to improve. After all, Ted Williams was one of the greatest players ever to put on a uniform. The last major leaguer to hit over .400, Williams possessed that rare combination of bat control and power. Observers assumed that those skills would rub off on his team. It didn't work out that way. When Williams took over the Senators they were a lousy team, and when he left they were still a lousy team. Somehow his own abilities as a player were not transferred to the players he managed. Even though he was a tremendous student of the game, his inborn gifts prevented him from fully appreciating what less gifted players needed. What came naturally for him, came painstakingly for them, or did not come at all.

"Are you a good preacher?" an incredulous colleague

asked, upon hearing that I had written a book on the subject. After some hesitation I replied, "No, I wouldn't claim that, but I'm getting better." Good preaching is elusive. To a large degree, it depends upon personality and innate gifts. Yet preaching can be improved through careful attention to purpose and technique. In some instances, preaching can be utterly revolutionized by a new approach. I have developed a new approach to my own preaching—storytelling—and it seems to have helped me. Perhaps those who read these pages can find new insights that will help their preaching, too.

This book is founded on the conviction that sermons can be improved through the skillful use of stories. More fundamentally, it is based on the premise that storytelling is a vital component to sermon effectiveness. I make this observation not solely on the basis of academic research but primarily from the humble experience of listening to sermons. I discovered in my early years as a sermon listener, during adolescence, that if I remembered anything at all from the sermons I heard, it was invariably the stories. I also noticed that sermons with good stories in them were both easier and more enjoyable to listen to. Regrettably, those discoveries are largely ignored by much formal homiletical training.

In some seminary courses on preaching, and in many homiletic texts (with the obvious exception of those cited in the bibliography), the emphasis is not on storytelling. Rather, the focus is likely to be on achieving a correct exegesis of the Scripture or infusing the sermon with proper theological content. Some attention may be given to organization or delivery, but those are often lesser concerns. My goal here is to elevate the importance of sermonic technique. No matter how vital the content, if it is not communicated in a clear and memorable way, the sermon will achieve little. In fact, some sermons which are biblically correct and even theologically profound are nonetheless boring. Thus, equal attention must be given to the sermon's form, style, and intentionality. It's not just a matter of what we say but also how we say it. That is where storytelling comes in. If my own experience as a sermon listener is any indication, stories can be powerful vehicles of truth. In short, the effective use of stories in preaching yields better sermons.

The thrust of this book is twofold: why and how to tell stories in sermons. First, the *why*. Without an adequate rationale for storytelling in preaching, there is little need for suggestions about how to do it. Hence, the first part of the book seeks to establish a rationale for using stories in sermons. Chapter 1 presents an overview of numerous obstacles to preaching, with the implicit notion that storytelling can somehow help to overcome them. Chapter 2 explores what stories can do to facilitate effective communication. Chapters 3 and 4 address the second concern of the book: how to tell stories. Specific guidelines are offered for storytelling in general and for the more precise application of using stories in sermons. Chapters 5, 6, and 7 contain sermons which illustrate the actual implementation of stories in preaching. Chapter 8 discusses criteria for evaluating stories and sermons. Chapter 9 addresses some specific questions about storytelling in preaching. Finally, the book concludes in chapter 10 with an assessment of the value of storytelling for preaching.

It was J. R. R. Tolkien, I believe, who coined that wonderful term *eucatastrophe*. He used it to connote a sudden, unexpected, joyous, miraculous turn of grace. As such, it is a "good catastrophe," a positive upheaval, a marvelous inbreaking of blessing. According to Tolkien,

The Birth of Christ is the eucatastrophe of Man's history. The Resurrection is the eucatastrophe of the story of the Incarnation. This story begins and ends in joy.[1]

Preaching is essentially an effort to communicate, transmit, transfer that experience of eucatastrophe. We do it by retelling the Story and by translating the experience of the Story into our own stories. The hope for mediocre preachers is simply that the eucatastrophe of the gospel is a repeatable event. Whenever the Story is told, and retold through lesser stories, eucatastrophe can happen again.

Note

1. J. R. R. Tolkien, *The Tolkien Reader* (New York: Ballantine Books, 1966), p. 71.

1
Once Upon a Time

God created man because He loves stories.
—Elie Wiesel[1]

Introduction

It was the summer after my freshman year in college. The four previous summers I had spent my vacation working in a laundry-and-dry-cleaning plant in Texas, but this year was different. I traveled to the state of Washington to work as a volunteer summer missionary. The assignment included everything from landscaping a church lawn to leading an outdoor Vacation Bible School in a town park. Toward the end of the summer, my supervisor asked me if I wanted to preach. I had never preached before, and I really did not know how to prepare and deliver a sermon, but something within me said yes.

The appointed Sunday came. It was an inauspicious occasion. I was so nervous that my tongue got twisted at least a dozen times. I had selected one familiar verse for my text because it seemed to have three main points. All I needed to do was elaborate on each one a bit, and then tack on a poem. The Scripture was Luke 9:23: "If any man will come after me, let him deny himself, and take up his cross daily, and follow me." No doubt, after listening to me mumble and stumble and bumble my way through the sermon, there were some who felt they had borne a cross that morning. Mercifully, the sermon was over in less than twelve minutes. I was not sure whether to feel humiliated or relieved. Yet, incredibly, every one of those seventy-five or so hearty souls who had endured my preaching filed out of the auditorium, shook my hand, and thanked me for coming. A few even found something complimentary to say about the sermon. It was my first taste of the pain and the glory that is preaching.

In his classic work *The Idea of the Holy,* Rudolf Otto characterized the apprehension of God as *mysterium tremendum.*[2] By that Otto meant that the experience of God provokes in us diverse, almost contradictory, feelings. We react with awe, but also with fascination in relationship to the holy. There is both an attraction and a fear, a mystery and a terror, a sense of wonder and a sense of unworthiness. That confluence of emotions approximates my feelings toward preaching. It is at once a fascinating and a terrifying enterprise. Robert Duke describes preaching as "an enormous responsibility, an exhilarating burden, and a dreadful opportunity."[3] To dare to speak of God, much less for God, is indeed an awesome calling.

Preaching is difficult. I discovered that the first time I tried to prepare a sermon. I rediscover that truth virtually every week as a pastor. Each time I sit before a blank tablet, or a computer terminal, and begin recording ideas for a new sermon, I marvel at my audacity. "Do I have what it takes to produce a worthwhile sermon?" I'm not alone in that feeling of natural hesitancy. Some of the most eminent preachers of this century, some of the pulpit greats, have also been plagued by self-doubts. George Buttrick wrote, "Preaching is in one regard like bringing up children: we know all about it until we have to do it; then we know nothing."[4] Harry Emerson Fosdick said,

"Preaching for me has never been easy."[5] William Barclay confessed, "All my life I have regarded preaching with dread. . . . For me to enter a pulpit has always been a literally terrifying experience."[6] It is no wonder that lesser preachers approach the pulpit with trepidation.

There are inherent difficulties in preaching itself which ought to make us think twice before we enter the pulpit. As Norman Mailer once remarked, "The sermon is a difficult art form, like a sonnet."[7] There are many formal limitations. It's not like writing free verse where anything goes. The preacher must be faithful to the text, sensitive to the needs of the congregation, aware of the liturgical tradition which provides the worship context. Time is limited, attention spans are limited, tolerance for new concepts is limited. Moreover, the preacher must assume many roles simultaneously. He is composer and performer, playwright and actor, poet and prophet. He cannot simply recite what someone else has written. He must create something new, both in the privacy of his study and on the public platform of a pulpit. Within this forum, the opportunities for naked failure are great. Sunday comes, and whether the preacher is ready or not, the people expect a word from the Lord.

Obstacles to Preaching

There are many obstacles to preaching. Not only is the sermon a difficult art form, the setting of the sermon makes preaching more difficulty. We must reckon with those who will hear our sermons. Preachers are not like the reclusive poet Emily Dickinson who wrote her poems only for herself and a few close friends, never intending that they should reach a wider audience. We prepare sermons for ourselves, of course, but for more than ourselves. Sermons are public events, directed toward specific persons with specific needs, interests, problems, and predispositions. When we take into account the intended audience, we find the preaching task ever more complex. Who are these people? Terry Young lists six characteristics common to many folk who listen to today's sermons.

1. They are pleasure oriented.
2. They have a scientific bent of mind.
3. They are pragmatic.
4. They are sales resistant.
5. They are money plagued.
6. They are accustomed to polished performances.[8]

When we consider these predispositions, we realize that not just any sermon will do. Sermons of even a generation ago may seem antiquated or irrelevant to people today. The complexities of modern life in the latter part of the twentieth century have vastly complicated the setting in which we preach. In short, our cultural context has created numerous obstacles to preaching. There are certainly more, but at least five obstacles seem especially challenging to modern preachers. In order to understand how preaching can be done at all in the present situation, let us look at these five dilemmas.

The Familiarity of the Gospel

I have a friend who pastors a Presbyterian church up the road. He recently lamented about how many sermons his people have heard him preach. He has been at the church twelve years, and he calculated that during that time some of "the faithful" have heard him preach over five-hundred times. "Imagine," he said, "five-hundred sermons! What can I possibly say to them that they have not heard before?"

It's a good question, and one possible explanation for

the relatively short tenure of many pastors. A sizable number of our congregants probably have heard it all before, if not from us, then from previous preachers. It is not as if we are sharing a new message. Even those who may not be regular churchgoers have an inkling of what the preacher is going to say. You can hardly live in America and not pick up smatterings of the gospel. A religious culture, a "Christian land," may, in fact, desensitize the populace to the radical newness of the Christian message. Still, because of our culture, the general details of the Christian faith are known. For those who have studied their Bibles and have listened attentively to sermons for years, the problem is even more acute. What can be said to them that they have not heard before? Even the most profound and eloquent of statements become clichés.

The Strangeness of the Biblical World View

George Gershwin's folk opera *Porgy and Bess,* introduced in 1935, reflects in some respects the mindset of the twentieth-century. Based upon a story by Dubose Heyward, the musical traces the lives of a community of poor blacks in Charleston, South Carolina. It is not only a commentary on the injustice of a segregated social system, but it is also a challenge to much other traditional wisdom and authority. The song "It Ain't Necessarily So" questions whether we can believe on a literal level everything we read in the Scriptures.

Much of the Bible seems incredible to the modern mind; many features seem strange and even unbelieveable. Angels, demons, animal sacrifice, a three-tiered universe—these are but a few of the ideas from that prescientific world. There is a fundamental difference between the cosmology of the Bible and our own. We no longer conceive of the earth as flat, with heaven above

and sheol below. We do not attribute every illness or
misfortune to the intrusion of spiritual forces. We do not
try to manipulate the gods, or God, through animal sac-
rifices or magic. Our scientific understandings of the
world have changed drastically since biblical times.

Further, our physical surroundings have changed, too.
Not only are the underlying assumptions about the work-
ings of the cosmos different, but the tangible elements of
daily life are technologically eons apart. Most of us do not
live on primitive farms in Palestine. For the biblical message to ring true in our urban culture, some transposition
is absolutely essential. A gospel from a setting of ox carts
and cow chips must be related to people more acquainted
with jet aircraft and computer chips. With every advance-
ment of modern society, the world view of the Bible
grows ever more distant. That fundamental strangeness
must somehow be overcome if we are ever to expect the
message of the Bible to be heard today.

The Distance Between the Pulpit and the Pew

Another obstacle to preaching is the gap in understanding between the clergy and the laity. A number of factors
make this breach almost inevitable. In many respects, the
minister and the parishioner operate on different planes.
First, there is a physical chasm between the preacher and
the people as the sermon is delivered. The preacher is set
apart, sometimes by vestments or title, most often by an
elevated pulpit. Physically and symbolically we are not on
the same level. Second, the preacher is usually paid to
preach. Unlike those in the pews who come to worship
without financial remuneration, the church is the preacher's job. That, too, diminishes solidarity with the people.

Preachers often speak a different language. Seminary
does that to a person. So do denominational associations

and relationships with other religious professionals. We learn theological terms which are not household words. We develop a kind of "church speak" which is largely unintelligible to the average person on the street. The temptation to use those technical terms and religious code words is almost irresistible. The words we speak can distance us from people in the pews.

Even if the preacher does refrain from religious jargon, his theological understanding is probably deeper than the layperson's. You would expect that. Years of theological study should have an effect. But there is no room for spiritual arrogance here. The preacher may know a lot about life in the Bible, but the layperson knows a lot about life in the world. Almost inevitably, the layperson's grasp of secular life is broader than the preacher's. After all, most ministers live in a rather protected environment. The majority of the preacher's daily social contacts are with church members or with other religious personnel. In contrast, many laypeople move and work in largely pagan surroundings. Those different spheres of experience tend to reduce commonality. Thus, the distance between pulpit and pew is an obstacle to preaching.

The Emphasis on Rational Argument

Another obstacle to preaching is the emphasis of Western culture on rational argument. We place great stress on reason and logic. As a consequence, the majority of our preaching assumes that logic alone is persuasive. Thus, the goal of much preaching is simply the transmission of information. Richard Jensen called it "didactic" preaching.[9] Such didactic sermons are primarily religious lectures, intended to make points and communicate ideas. The result is a preaching tradition which approaches Scripture with the same empiricist agenda that the scien-

tist brings to the laboratory. The components of the text
are separated and broken down into their constituent
parts, and a sermon is developed around a reasonable
thesis with an ordered progression of logical ideas.

How did this method of sermonizing get started? Apparently, very early in the church's history, the narrative
tradition of the Bible was subsumed under the Greek
tradition of discursive rhetoric. The impact of Greek
thought on early Christian preaching was carried over
into preaching today. Al Fasol concluded that "the roots
of Christian preaching may lie in Hebrew history, but the
form of Christian preaching is indelibly influenced by
Greek rhetoric."[10] Don Wardlaw made much the same
point when he said, "Church fathers from Origen to
Chrysostom, while imbued with the mind of Christ, exegeted and preached with the mind of Plato and Aristotle."[11] Because this Hellenizing influence happened so
early in the church's history, subsequent preachers failed
to grasp this transformation. With few exceptions, preachers have been reluctant to leapfrog over centuries of
homiletical history to return to the biblical emphasis on
storytelling.

But is rationally centered preaching necessarily bad? Is
a focus on logic and reason necessarily an impediment to
preaching? If it has served churches well for this long,
what is the problem? Obviously, some amount of reasoning is essential for any discourse. The problem is the assumption that the aims of preaching are achieved solely,
or even most effectively, through rational argument. Simply put, information itself is not persuasive. Nor is the will
automatically motivated by mere intellectual assent. For
example, mounting scientific evidence has shown conclu-
sively that cigarette smoking is harmful to health. Still, in
spite of the convincing logic not to do so, many people

continue to smoke. Apparently, something more is needed than sheer logic. For people to quit smoking, they must become gripped with a vision of life that can provide them with the motivation to change their life-styles.

The aim of the sermon is similar—not just to get people to stop smoking, but more completely, to motivate people to change their lives. If preaching is to succed on that level, sermons must employ those means which are most effective in modifying or replacing the deep images we live by. Reason may appeal to the mind, but volitional commitment involves the emotions and the will.

An Oral Medium in a Visual Context

One final obstacle for preaching today is the impact of television, motion pictures, videos, computer games, and other visual media on sermon listening. Given the sensory bombardment that most of us are exposed to in the course of daily living, the sermon can seem like a rather dull affair. Even with a microphone, how can the small, shrill voice of the preacher be heard amidst the profusion of competing sounds and images which swirls about us?

The odds seem overwhelming. Persons who spend fifty hours a year listening to sermons spend fifty hours a week watching television. People have grown so accustomed to instant entertainment, to easy involvement, and to graphic information that the typical sermon seems woefully ill-equipped to make any lasting impression. How can a medium which is basically oral compete in a visual context?

One answer has been the rise of the electronic church. Some preachers have concluded that one way to make sermons more exciting is to put them on television. Thus, there has been a veritable explosion of television evangelists in recent years. Financial constraints may limit that growth, but in most church situations televised preaching is not practicable or even desirable. I have a hunch that people would soon rebel if we asked them to come to church and watch a television monitor on the pulpit instead of a real, live person. Still, there is no going back—the *eyes* have it. And unless a sermon can help people "see," it likely will not help them at all.

Toward a Possible Solution

These obstacles to preaching are not insurmountable. Storytelling in preaching can help to overcome each impediment. Stories can bring new life to a gospel message which is otherwise all too familiar. Stories can help to bridge the distance between the world view of the Bible and our own. Stories can reduce or even eliminate the distance between the pulpit and the pew. Stories can serve as a balancing corrective to an overemphasis on rational argument by appealing to the emotions and the will. Stories can function effectively in a visual context because they enable people to see with the mind, imagination, and heart. In short, using stories as illustrations in sermons can lead to more effective preaching.

Did the young preacher who so mangled his first sermon give up? No, for even though it was a painful and largely failed experience, I caught a glimpse of what preaching could be. Today, nearly two decades later, I am still at it. Some Sundays I almost shudder as I stand at the back door of the sanctuary after the worship service, fully aware of how far short my best efforts for that day have fallen. But every now and then, there comes some confirmation that the words which passed my lips reached responsive ears and hearts. A squeeze of the hand, a tear in the eye, a phone call later in the week with a compliment about the sermon which is not so much a compliment as a confession. Every now and then, I dare to believe it made a difference. Like that one true shot out of a hundred errant ones on the golf course, it is enough to bring you back next week to try again.

Notes

1. Elie Wiesel, *The Gates of the Forest* (New York: Avon Books, 1967), p. 10.

2. Rudolf Otto, *The Idea of the Holy*, trans. John W. Harvey (London: Oxford University Press, 1950), pp. 12.

3. Robert W. Duke, *The Sermon as God's Word* (Nashville: Abingdon, 1980), p. 112.

4. George A. Buttrick, *Jesus Came Preaching* (New York: Charles Scribner's Sons, 1931), p. x.

5. Harry Emerson Fosdick, *The Living of These Days* (New York: Harper & Row, Publishers, 1956), p. 84.

6. William Barclay, *A Spiritual Autobiography* (Grand Rapids: William B. Eerdmans Publishing Company, 1975), p. 72.

7. Clyde Reid, *The Empty Pulpit* (New York: Harper & Row, Publishers, 1967), p. 47.

8. J. Terry Young, "Pastor, What Was that You Said?" *Proclaim*, 8 (April-May-June 1978), p. 44.

9. Richard A. Jensen, *Telling the Story* (Minneapolis: Augsburg Publishing House, 1980), p. 11.

10. Al Fasol, *A Guide to Self-Improvement in Sermon Delivery* (Grand Rapids: Baker Book House, 1983), p. 11.

11. Don M. Wardlaw, *Preaching Biblically: Creating Sermons in the Shape of Scripture* (Philadelphia: The Westminster Press, 1983), p. 11.

2
Tell Me the Story

The destiny of the world is determined less by the battles that are lost and won than by the stories it loves and believes in. Stories are told, grow old, and are remembered. Battles are fought, fade out, and are forgotten—unless they beget great stories.

—Harold C. Goddard[1]

Scripture as Story

Storytelling is profoundly biblical. There is an amazing amount of narrative material within Holy Scriptures. Amos Wilder maintains that stories are uniquely important to the Judeo-Christian tradition.

If one looks at other religious and philosophical classics the story aspects may be relatively marginal. Their sacred books may often rather take the form of philosophical instruction or mystical treatise or didactic code or oracular vision.[2]

Within the Bible, however, it is story which is prominent. A narrative thread runs throughout, an underlying plot giving thematic unity to the whole. Most of us were introduced to the Bible through its stories. Even before we grasped an underlying theme in Scripture, we heard individual stories which invaded our imaginations and found permanent niches in our memories.

The Old Testament is a treasure book of stories. Perhaps that is because story is the most easily transmitted literary form. Before words were ever recorded on parchment or paper, stories were told orally from fathers to sons—generation to generation. Stories could be remembered and repeated with astounding accuracy because good stories are naturally memorable. Certainly, the Old Testament includes a variety of genres, such as laws, proverbs, songs, genealogies, and prophetic oracles. Yet it is story which provides the larger framework into which those other forms are integrated.

But why did the biblical writers resort so often to stories? Why, for example, did not the author of Genesis simply tell us what sin is, instead of telling us a story about it?[3] Could it be that the ancient writers realized almost intuitively the unique powers of narrative? Not only are stories remembered, they carry an evocative force beyond that of simple declarative statements. One factor in this evocative force is the way in which stories draw us into the tales. We identify with the characters, we feel the suspense, we get caught up in the action, we resonate with the plot. Eventually, in some way the biblical story becomes our story. In the process, Scripture becomes forever contemporary, so that even in the midst of different historical circumstances, the story speaks forcefully to each new age.

Stories are also important in the New Testament. Look at the Gospels—basically stories about Jesus. Look at the teachings of Jesus—sayings, yes, like the Sermon on the Mount, but also stories in the form of parables. Jesus recognized the value of storytelling in His own preaching and teaching. Especially in the Synoptic Gospels, the sto-

ries of Jesus play a highly significant role. Sometimes the
parables are interpreted within the Gospels, such as the
parable of the seed and the soils. More often, the parables
were simply recorded by the Gospel writers and allowed
to stand alone without further amplification. Apparently
the writers trusted the stories because Jesus trusted the
stories to convey truth. When we consider the amount of
narrative material from the lips of Jesus and surrounding
His life, the whole category of story takes on new significance. Add to that the stories from the Book of Acts, and
the stories upon which many of the Epistles are based,
and we recognize that stories are a major literary form of
the New Testament.

Robert Waznak remarked that Christianity began as a
community of storytellers. The earliest order of worship
was something akin to "gather the folk, break the bread,
and tell the stories."[4] A rediscovery of storytelling may
signal a return to biblical roots.

Stories and Human Experience

It is difficult to overstate the role of story in the propaga-
tion of culture. Storytelling, in some form, is probably as
old as human speech. John Harrell contended that prehis-
toric man, as early as a hundred thousand years ago, was
capable of developed language and began informal storytelling.[5] Ruth Sawyer suggested that the first efforts at
conscious storytelling consisted of impromptu chants, ex-
tolling some act of bravery by a member of the tribe.[6] In
whatever form, stories served to organize and order culture. From the very beginning, humans have felt a need
to recount their experiences. Stories were of course entertaining, but even more, stories served to picture life as
part of a meaningful whole. "Preliterate man lived in a
world which received its intellectual, religious, and social

structure through the story."[7] Through narrative, ancient peoples preserved and presented their understandings of reality.

Stories are essential not just to societies but also to families and individuals. Whether around the campfire or the dinner table, we tell stories to communicate our life experiences. We also interpret our experiences through those larger patterns of understanding passed on to us. We use stories to help us comprehend the meaning of events. Stories carry the images, motifs, and fundamental patterns by which we organize and engage reality.

Stories in Preaching

In addition to biblical and cultural rationales, there is also a homiletical rationale for telling stories in sermons. Storytelling is, in fact, integral to preaching. On what basis do I make that claim? The process of sermon development. Every preacher must develop a procedure for preparing sermons. Most sermons do not just happen via "stream of consciousness." Occasionally a sermon will take shape in a dream or daydream, but we would do best not to depend upon that method of inspiration. Generally, we move through definite stages in sermon composition. As we move through those stages, the need for a narrative dimension becomes more obvious. At the risk of oversimplification, I am suggesting a three-step process for sermon development. This process reveals why storytelling is integral to preaching. The three steps are audience analysis, demythologizing the text, and remythologizing the message.

Step 1: The Pastoral Imperative—Audience Analysis

Fundamental to preaching is identifying and indentifying with the audience. It is not enough simply to know and understand the Scriptures. We must know and understand our people as well. The interpretation of a Scripture passage depends, to some degree, on the concrete circumstances into which that message is given. This is the meeting place of the text and the people. Hence, there is a symbiotic relationship between the message we proclaim and those to whom we proclaim it. This has always been so.

Serious students of the New Testament have long recognized this relationship between text and people. For example, why do the Synoptic Gospels, which contain much of the same material, differ in certain details and in terms of thematic emphasis? Was it the faulty memories of the writers? Not at all. Many of the differences between Matthew, Mark, and Luke are due to the differences between their intended readers. The audiences determined the shape of the Gospels. In some instances, one author may have had information not available to the others. But the major reason for the different Gospels is that the inspired writers wrote with specific readers in mind. Each Gospel has a slightly different emphasis because each was addressed to a slightly different situation.

Joachim Jeremias noted that this impact of the intended audience affects the interpretation of the parables. Many of the parables of Jesus were originally addressed to a hostile audience—the Pharisees, the scribes, or the crowd. Later those same parables were addressed by the primitive church to the followers of Jesus. Thus, the parables in their present form reflect this adaptation to specific congregations. Jeremias further defended this hortatory application, not as a misinterpretation but rather as the actualization of the text.[8] That same actualizing process must be used in sermons today. What is to be said in the sermon is largely determined by what the people need to hear.

How do we know what message the people need? H. H. Farmer suggested there are two sets of influences or conditions which work to shape the life of every person.[9] One set of factors is the unchanging, internal needs which all of us have. These are those permanent, universal conditions: suffering, bereavement, fear, guilt, and so on. The other conditions, however, are the more particular external influences of environment, variables which are characteristic of a specific age, culture, or subculture. Thus, both universal and particular needs must be considered in the analysis of the audience.

This explains why a sermon of even a generation ago may seem terribly dated. Times change, attitudes change, concerns change. Biblical truth is constant, but its actualization must remain fluid. For this reason, Welton Gaddy cautioned against trying to present a "timeless" message. Such an aim will doubtless lead to irrelevant abstractions. He said "Abstractness and timelessness stand as two of the greatest curses of preaching."[10] The irony is that the preacher who tries to be timeless will be abstract while the preacher who addresses the specific needs of people may be timeless. Only as we get in touch with the real-life stories of our people will we be able to comprehend how the biblical story can apply to their needs. In order to prepare people to hear the Story, we must understand how it corresponds with their personal narratives. Only then can the stories we tell function as a kind of "mirror" through which people can interpret their own life dramas.

What does this mean in terms of sermon preparation? It means there is no substitute for pastoral visitation. This past year I set as a goal for myself to visit in the home of every family in our congregation. Because ours is a small church, that was a feasible aim. I set aside two evenings each week and made pastoral calls. The results were gratifying. I got to know people on a level not possible in the usual Sunday morning setting. I heard personal stories and discovered personal needs that I would not have known about otherwise. Obviously, I did not translate these visits directly into sermons. That would have betrayed confidences and undermined the purpose of the visits. But I did use those visitation experiences to help me to analyze my congregation on an ongoing basis. And that audience analysis contributed to the process of sermon development.

Step 2: The Exegetical Task—Hearing the Text

Along with exegeting the people, the second part of the homiletical equation is an exegesis of the biblical text. I am describing this exegetical task as "hearing the text." But first, let us examine the goals of exegesis. William Thompson has drawn a helpful distinction between exegesis and hermeneutics, terms which are sometimes used interchangeably. *Exegesis,* according to Thompson, is a study to discover what the biblical writer meant and how that meaning was understood by the original readers. Conversely, the main thrust of hermeneutics is discovering the biblical meaning for today.[11] As such, *hermeneutics* is a more comprehensive concept, moving beyond an exegesis of the text to an exegesis of the current situation and a translation of the text's meaning into contemporary language and thought patterns. All of this is to say that while exegesis is foundational to preaching, it is only one step in the sermon preparation process. Exegesis is an attempt to hear the text, but it must be followed by her-

meneutical efforts to express the meaning of the text
through the proclamation of the sermon.

Harry Emerson Fosdick, in his important 1930 book
The Modern Use of the Bible, sought to draw a distinction
between "man's abiding experiences and their temporary
expressions."[12] Fosdick saw the preacher's job as that
of decoding the abiding meanings of the Bible from
their ancient phraseology. The net result was a method
of understanding the Bible's message by going
through the "ephemeral category" into the "repeatable
experience."[13] This method of interpretation is based on
the assumption that there is a continuity of human experience and perception which is transcultural and transgen-
erational. In other words, there is an abiding truth in
Scripture not bound by cultural trappings. It is the task of
exegesis to identify that common experience within the
text and to separate it from those archaic expressions
which mask its meaning. This is the process which I have
described as "hearing the text."

Step 3: The Hermeneutical Necessity—Contemporizing the Text

Hearing the text is an important, but penultimate, task.
Sermon preparation is not finished until the larger her-
meneutical work has been done, namely that of contemporizing the message. Since every idea, concept, or truth
is time conditioned, it is impossible to present the essence
of the text apart from some cultural wrapping. Deane
Kemper believes that exegesis comprises about one third
of the effort necessary to produce a worthwhile sermon.[14]
The remaining two thirds of the work must be spent on
translating the content of the message into a contemporary idiom. The meaning of the text must be given new
expression for each new telling. Amos Wilder

has pointed out that with the passage of time, all communication changes. Only things like the multiplication table can be recited without translation. "To merely reproduce the words of the New Testament," Wilder said, "is to falsify their original meaning and to defraud modern hearers of that meaning."[15] Somehow that meaning must be recast in fresh and evocative ways.

How does this contemporizing take place? Just as the early writers transformed the materials available to them into distinctive Gospels designed to meet the needs of their local communities, so preachers today adapt their resources (the Bible) in light of their congregations.[16] Similarly, Clyde Francisco argued that since the authors of Scripture used the cultural materials of their day, "we should be free to use own our cultural expressions to declare to our generation the same truth proclaimed by the biblical writers."[17] Far from being a violation of the text, this is precisely how the church has always used the Bible to speak to each new age. Christian truth must be forever actualized in each new context, with dynamic analogies, contemporary descriptions, provocative juxtapositions, and yes, new stories.

To speak of contemporizing then, is to speak of *restorying* the gospel. Propositional statements may be necessary for theology, for exegesis, but they are not adequate for preaching. To say, "You are forgiven," or "God loves you," apart from the biblical story is almost meaningless. Similarly, to simply repeat the biblical story without making contact with our stories is not enough. But to connect the biblical events with the nitty-gritty happenings of our lives, ah, that is occasion for grace!

Dare we suggest that preaching is nothing more than storytelling? No. Just as the Bible contains literary forms other than narrative, so preaching must incorporate other

modes of communication. Despite the ground swell of
enthusiasm for narrative preaching in recent years, there
are limits to the use of stories in preaching. Chester Pennington noted, for example, that the gospel story raises
questions which cannot be adequately answered solely by
more stories.[18] Rather, preaching must include both stories and explanations, both narrative to evoke and discursive statements to explain. It is the actual use of stories in
sermons which is the focus of the following chapters.

Notes

1. Harold C. Goddard, *The Meaning of Shakespeare*, vol. 2 (Chicago: The University of Chicago Press, 1960), p. 208.

2. Amos Wilder, *Early Christian Rhetoric: The Language of the Gospel* (Cambridge: Harvard University Press, 1964), p. 56.

3. Jensen, *Telling the Story*, (Minneapolis: Augsburg Publishing House, 1980), p. 128.

4. Robert Waznak, *Sunday after Sunday: Preaching the Homily as Story* (New York: Paulist Press, 1983), p. 27.

5. John Harrell, *Origins and Early Traditions of Storytelling* (Kensington, California: York House, Publishers, 1983), p. 10.

6. Ruth Sawyer, *The Way of the Storyteller* (New York: Viking Press, 1942), pp. 45-46.

7. Sam Keen, *To a Dancing God* (New York: Harper & Row, Publishers, 1970), p. 87.

8. Joachim Jeremias, *The Parables of Jesus*, 2nd rev. ed. (New York: Charles Scribner's Sons, 1972), p. 48.

9. Herbert H. Farmer, *The Servant of the Word* (Philadelphia: Fortress Press, 1964), pp. 84-85.

10. C. Welton Gaddy, "Preaching that Communicates," *Search*, 4 (Winter 1974), p. 14.

11. William D. Thompson, *Preaching Biblically: Exegesis and Interpretation* (Nashville: Abingdon, 1981), pp. 15-38.

12. Harry Emerson Fosdick, *The Modern Use of the Bible* (New York: The Macmillan Company, 1930), p. 55.

13. Ibid., p. 169.

14. Deane A. Kemper, *Effective Preaching: A Manual for Students and Pastors* (Philadelphia: The Westminster Press, 1985), p. 10.

15. Wilder, *Early Christian Rhetoric*, pp. 122-123.

16. William E. Hull, "Preaching on the Synoptic Gospels," *Biblical Preaching: An Expositor's Treasury*, ed. James W. Cox (Philadelphia: The Westminster Press, 1983), p. 175.

17. Clyde T. Francisco, "Preaching from the Primeval Narrativies of Genesis," *Biblical Preaching: An Expositor's Treasury*, ed. James W. Cox (Philadelphia: The Westminster Press, 1983), p. 18.

18. Chester A. Pennington, "Response to 'Preaching and Story,'" *The Iliff Review*, 37 (Fall 1980), p. 64.

3
The Art of Storytelling

A rabbi, whose grandfather had been a disciple of the Baal Shem, was asked to tell a story. "A story," he said, "must be told in such a way that it constitutes help in itself." And he told: "My grandfather was lame. Once they asked him to tell a story about his teacher. And he related how the holy Baal Shem used to hop and dance while he prayed. My grandfather rose as he spoke, and he was so swept away by the story that he himself began to hop and dance to show how the master had done. From that hour on he was cured of his lameness. That's the way to tell a story!"

—Martin Buber[1]

Storytelling as an Art Form

It was Samuel Taylor Coleridge who provided the classic definition of art: the immediate object is pleasure, and the ultimate object is truth.[2] Under that definition, stories are an art form. There is something pleasurable about a good story. Television programmers have discovered that if you want people to sit in front of a picture tube for hours on end, you must tell them stories. Television is a storytelling medium. Movies, prime-time dramatic series, soap operas, situation comedies, game shows, sports, the news, even commercials—all are basically stories. They are interesting, entertaining, involving, pleasurable. But good stories do not merely entertain. Like all genuine art, good stories convey truth. They convey truth because they provide us with a picture of reality. Frederick Buechner wrote:

> The storyteller's claim, I believe, is that life has meaning. The power of stories is that they are telling us that life adds up somehow, that life itself is like a story. And this grips us and fascinates us because of the feeling it gives us that if there is meaning in any life—in Hamlet's, in Mary's, in Christ's—then there is meaning also in our lives.[3]

It is the possibility that stories can somehow illumine our own lives which gives stories their attraction and power. Researchers have found that many people say they watch television soap operas in order to find answers to their own problems.[4] Stories allow us to reflect upon our own stories, as well as to vicariously experience other modes of behavior and perception. Paul Flucke said that "the value of a well-shaped story is that its action and characters 'resonate' with something in the listener's own experience."[5] Sometimes this happens without intention. We are drawn into the tale out of curiosity, and before we know it, we are drawing comparisons between the events of the story and ourselves. Eugene Lowry explained this phenomenon when he said:

> Anytime you tell a story, you open the door for metaphor to operate. When, for example, you describe the apprehension a child experiences in moving to a new school, you have done more than describe moving to a new school. You have produced a metaphor that touches images of apprehension throughout the congregation. You may not have intended to address that person who is about to retire from the railroad . . . and that person may not be able to

identify just what the connection was, but impact—however undefined propositionally—happened.[6]

Stories may be able to teach, console, and persuade more effectively than any other form of communication. Stories can focus experience even more forcefully than actual events. Thus, we may learn more vicariously from a story in the span of a few minutes than we learn experientially from life in the span of months or years. What begins in pleasure ends in truth.

Characteristics of a Good Story

What is it that makes a particular story good? Quite simply, something must happen. There must be some tension, some ambiguity, some twist, some unforeseen turning, some threat, or some surprise. If the story is to arouse our interest and maintain our attention, there must be some element of contingency. But there's more. The characters, plot, and conclusion of the story must have the ring of truth. This is not to suggest that every story must masquerade as actual event. Even fantasy can have the ring of truth if the motivations and behavior of the characters are believable. The opportunity for identification is the key. In good stories, we are able to identify with one or more of the characters. If no one in the story matters to us, the outcome of the story will not matter either.

How do you write a good story? A number of writers have suggested stylistic principles for good narratives. The following list includes characteristics which most writers would include as qualities of a good story:

1. A single, clearly defined theme
2. A single perspective from which the story develops
3. A well-formed plot which moves from calm to conflict to resolution

4. A use of realistic, graphic detail
5. An appeal to the senses whenever possible
6. A few major characters; lesser characters described only as necessary to the action
7. A reliance on direct speech; feelings and motives mentioned only when essential for the point
8. A judicious use of repetition, with end stress; that is, the most important thing is described last[7]

These guidelines are by no means exhaustive, but they do suggest that good stories involve proven techniques as well as creative artistry. How a story is related is just as important as what happens in the story. Good story form makes good story content enjoyable, even revelatory.

Preparing to Tell the Story

In most cases, story composition precedes storytelling. Whether the story is original or drawn from an outside source, it must be composed by the teller before it is told. In other words, the story must be plotted. Characters must be selected, events sequenced, descriptions visualized, and conclusions drawn. It matters little whether the story is written on paper or formulated in the mind. The process of story development is the same.

Using Suspense in Story Development

As has been mentioned, some element of contingency is essential for any story. Something unforeseen, unpredictable must happen. The story must develop suspense. This introduction of suspense differentiates a story from a report. A report simply links together a series of past events. A good storyteller, however, introduces tension, increases the tension, and then releases it at just the right moment.[8] Without that tension, there is little motivation to follow what is being told.

How is this tension introduced? It does not take much to arouse people's interest initially. Something like, "Several months ago I was on my way to . . ." and with those few words of introduction, the listeners are on their way, too. Something is about to be told them that they do not already know. This is the beginning of suspense. However, more information must be added to maintain interest. This initial tension must be stretched and swollen if the story is to progress.

One of the pioneers of modern storytelling, Marie Shedlock, warned about the dangers of side issues in story development.[9] An otherwise exciting story can be destroyed when tangential matters are introduced. It's true. I once knew a woman who could seldom get straight to the point of anything she said. It was frustrating to listen to her, even sad. Almost everything she said reminded her of something else. As a result, she could not finish any thought without jumping to another one. She had few friends, probably due in part to her schizophrenic pattern of communication. People simply lacked the patience to muddle through a series of disjointed thoughts in order to understand what she was saying.

Story development demands continuity and singleness of purpose. It is critical that the escalating ambiguity of a story not be diluted by additional characters or subplots. Thematic unity will not tolerate interruptions. Let the thirty-second television commercial, not the two-hour feature-length movie, be our guide.

Reaching a Turning Point or Climax

The resolution of ambiguity is the goal of most stories. Those stories which leave the listener "hanging" produce an indeterminate meaning. Occasionally, we might enjoy an open-ended the story where the final outcome is somewhat in doubt. More often we receive pleasure when the conflict is resolved. That is why it is so unsettling to turn off a television program before it is over or to put down a good book just before the climax. Only when the tension has been relieved can we experience the pleasure of the story's resolution. When suspense remains suspended, it is difficult to draw conclusions.

Paul Ricoeur wrote that "instead of being predictable, a conclusion must be acceptable."[10] The climax may be a suprise, but it must not be disjointed from the rest of the story. However unexpected, the final development must be continuous with what has gone before. It is this unpredictability, and acceptability, which allows the hearers to experience a collective "Aha!" at the moment of resolution. Then they may find that the unexpected is the most acceptable conclusion, even though they did not anticipate it. In fact, the only thing worse than a disjointed ending is an obvious ending. When we know how a story will end, there is little need to follow it all the way through.

Drawing Implications for Meaning

The application aspect of storytelling may be the most delicate art of all. On the one hand, the teller must trust the story to convey its meaning. On the other hand, the teller must recognize the inherent limitations of story as indirect discourse. It is, of course, a great mistake to simply hand the listener the truth of the story in a didactic way. It is true that some stories for children, such as Aesop's Fables, often conclude with a moral or lesson. Yet even children must be allowed to experience truth in the hearing. A detailed explanation can either reduce the meaning of the story, or overinterpret the meaning so that the affective force of the narrative is lost. Like jokes, when stories have to be explained, there is not much point in telling them. If the story is to speak, it must speak on its own terms. A storyteller would do well to hold off a bit and allow the story to be heard in all its complexity and power.

Having said all that, we must nonetheless acknowledge that for many stories some degree of interpretation is necessary. If that were not true, there would be no need for preaching. We could simply read stories from the Bible and go home. That might be OK for a while, but sooner or later people would begin to ask: "What do the stories mean for us?" The aim of preaching is not to rob the biblical narratives of their force, but rather to focus that force. This need for focusing becomes especially crucial when nonbiblical stories are used. Some connections between "secular" stories and the gospel must be made; otherwise, the sermon might be mistaken for an interesting lecture. There is always the chance that the listener will hear only the superficial action of the story. Likewise, the religious connotations of the story may be so subtle that the hearers feel stranded, struggling to discern the meaning or intent. Thus, in some way, the implications of the story must be applied to the situation of the listeners. This application should be very brief, perhaps even understated, but precise enough to point the hearers to what the story might mean for them.

Learning the Story

After the story has been composed, it must be learned for telling. Regardless of method of delivery—memorized, extemporaneous, notes, or manuscript—familiarity with the story is absolutely essential. Even if the story is read (and this is the least preferable method), it must be conveyed with enthusiasm, spontaneity, and freedom. A

number of storytellers caution against reading or memo-
rizing the story. Rather, the story should be told as if it
were a personal remembrance. Hence, the goal is not to
try to learn the story word for word, or even to tell it
flawlessly. Since the congregation does not know in advance what the preacher is going to say, they likely will
not be aware of missing details. Even the most seasoned
storytellers expect to make some mistakes. It is not mistakes but our negative reactions to them which detract
from storytelling.[11] If the hearers sense our embarrass-
ment, they will share it. But miscues need not destroy the
story. A crucial missing detail can be supplied later in the
telling while nonessential matters can be omitted altogether.

If the goal is to tell stories as if they were personal
reminiscences, how are those stories to be learned? Ruth
Sawyer advocated learning the story "incident by incident, picture by picture."[12] Like the frames of a comic
strip, the main movements of a story can be sequenced in
the mind. Or a few key words can be used to signal the
major points of the story. One storyteller I know, a public
librarian, rehearses her stories in front of a mirror before
she tells them. Another narrates her stories into a tape
recorder and plays the tape back while driving in her car.
Doubtless, every storyteller will have to develop personalized techniques for learning the story. This much is certain: only as we have mastered the story, and been
mastered by it, can the story come alive.

Notes

1. Martin Buber, *Tales of the Hasidim*, trans. Olga Marx (New York: Schock-
en Books, Inc., 1957), pp. v-vi.

2. Samuel Taylor Coleridge, *Selected Poetry and Prose of Coleridge*, ed. Donald A. Stauffer (n.p.: Random House, 1951), p. 267.

3. Frederick Buechner, *The Magnificent Defeat* (New York: The Seabury Press, 1966), p. 60.

4. Ralph L. Lewis and Gregg Lewis, *Inductive Preaching* (Westchester, Ill.: Crossway Books, 1983), p. 160.

5. Paul Flucke, "Can I Say It with a Story: The Story's Action and Characters 'Resonate' Something in the Listener's Own Experience," *The Christian Ministry*, 14 (Mar. 1983), p. 27.

6. Eugene L. Lowry, *Doing Time in the Pulpit* (Nashville: Abingdon, 1985), p. 91.

7. Rudolf Bultmann, *History of the Synoptic Tradition*, revd. ed., (New York: Harper & Row, Publishers, 1963), pp. 190-192.

8. James Limburg, *Old Testament Stories for a New Time* (Atlanta: John Knox Press, 1983), p. 27.

9. Marie L. Shedlock, *The Art of the Storyteller*, 3rd rev. ed. (New York: Dover Publications, Inc., 1951), p. 4.

10. Paul Ricoeur, "The Narrative Function," *Semeia*, 13 (1978), 182.

11. Daniel Juniper, *Along the Water's Edge: Stories that Challenge and How to Tell Them* (New York: Paulist Press, 1982), p. 103.

12. Sawyer, *Way of the Storyteller*, p. 142.

4
Doing Storytelling in Preaching

There is an old story of a boilermaker who was hired to fix a huge steamship boiler system. After listening to the engineer's description of the problems and asking a few questions, he went to the boiler room. He looked at the maze of twisting pipes, listened to the thump of the boiler and the hiss of escaping steam for a few minutes, and felt some pipes with his hands. Then he hummed softly to himself, reached into his overalls and took out a small hammer, and tapped a bright red valve, once. Immediately the entire system began working perfectly, and the boilermaker went home. When the steamship owner received a bill for $1000, he complained that the boilermaker had only been in the engine room for fifteen minutes, and requested an itemized bill.

FOR TAPPING WITH HAMMER   .50
FOR KNOWING WHERE TO TAP   <u>999.50</u>
                         $1000.00 TOTAL
             —Richard Bandler, John Grindler[1]

Using Stories in Sermons

We now come to the major focus of this book: using stories in sermons. The goal here is to show how stories may be used as sermon illustrations. This particular emphasis is to be distinguished from so-called "narrative preaching." Eugene Lowry, Edmund Steimle, Charles Rice, Henry Mitchell, Don Wardlaw, David Brown, Thomas Troeger, Richard Jensen, and others have written books in the last decade which conceive of preaching itself as storytelling. (See Bibliography, "Narrative Preaching".) Others like Fred Craddock and Ralph Lewis have advocated a closely related inductive approach to preaching. The focus of this book is in sympathy with, but not identical to, the concerns of narrative preaching. Herein lies the distinction. Whereas many of the proponents of narrative preaching advocate a story form for the sermon, this book conceives of stories being used in the more traditional way as sermon illustrations. My objective is not to refute narrative preaching—far from it. Rather, I simply want to demonstrate how stories can be used in almost any form of sermon to increase preaching effectiveness.

The use of stories as illustrations in sermons is certainly not a new idea. All too often, however, this device has become hackneyed and superficial. I am not talking about how to insert an occasional joke or anecdote into the sermon to make it more entertaining. That can be done, but you don't need to read a book about it. Instead, I am seeking to justify and redefine story as integral to preaching. My point is this: Illustrations are not expendable additions or dispensable afterthoughts to the sermon. Perhaps even the term *illustration* is misleading, especially as it is understood to be a secondary mode of communication. At the very least, illustrations stand on equal footing with the didactic, propositional statements that comprise the bulk of most sermons.

William Bausch says it exactly: "I do not want the stories to be seen as illustrations of the text. The stories are the text. All the rest is commentary."[2] If the stories we tell in sermons are secondary to anything, they are secondary not to our discursive comments but only to the biblical story. The conventional wisdom that illustrations are subordinate to declarative statements must be overturned. Both illustrations and declarative statements are subordinate to Scripture, and both are necessary to adequately interpret the meaning of Scripture for people today.

The Function of Stories in Sermons

Generally, stories serve the same functions as other types of sermon illustrations. They can be used to clarify what has been stated, to provide concrete examples of more general assertions, to allow for listener identification, and to provide relief—comic or dramatic—from rational arguments. Stories can achieve all of these purposes, and many more, according to how they are used.

In his book *Guide to Biblical Preaching*, James Cox made a precise distinction between two uses of illustrative material. He called these two basic forms "examples" and "illustrations." Cox wrote, "Examples are actual instances or cases that demonstrate a truth; illustrations are comparisons or stories that in some way resemble an aspect of a truth, help to clarify it, and thus serve to inform or move the hearer."[3]

Cox has actually described two of the primary ways that stories may be used in sermons. Stories may be used deductively as examples to demonstrate a truth, or they may be used inductively as illustrations to analogically point to a truth. Using the deductive approach, the preacher states a truth and then uses a story as an example to support the general proposition. Under the inductive approach, a story is told, and some aspect of the story is used analogically to move the hearer to a new level of understanding. In either case, the story works in tandem with the nonnarrative, analytical statements of the sermon to interpret, or remythologize, the biblical text.

When to Use Stories in Sermons

The placement of stories in sermons is crucial to their effectiveness. This placement involves how stories are used, and how often. Ian Macpherson's comment that "one illustration should be used to drive home each point of the sermon" should not be discarded hastily.[4] There is something to be said for a one-to-one correspondence between the major movements of a sermon and the stories. Notice I said *major movements* of the sermon, not points. I have seen sermon outlines with dozens of points. Were a different story to be used to illustrate each point of the outline, the sermon could last all day. I have read that it was not uncommon for Puritan divines to preach for two hours and then turn the sandglass over to begin an hour more. That might have worked in colonial America where people were required to go to church, but it probably would not work today.

Certainly, stories should be used judiciously. Using many short stories together makes the sermon should like one of those anecdotal pages out of *Reader's Digest*. Conversely, even a few longer stories may fight against one another. It takes discipline to consciously restrict the number of stories in a sermon, particularly when you have discovered how effective stories can be. But the law of "diminishing returns" is operative in homiletics. A few poignant stories, or even one, may have more impact than many piled on top of each other. Further, John Killinger advocated that the illustrative material be arranged so that the emotional level is ascending, not descending, as the sermon progresses.[5] In this way, stories work in harmony with one another to move the sermon toward its desired end.

How long should a story be? It should be no longer than necessary, but long enough to be told adequately. George Bass recommended the one-page short story as a good model, with the preacher attempting to reduce it even further if he can do so without violating its impact.[6] If stories are too brief, they do not allow the congregation to enter into them with any depth of participation. On the other hand, a long and involved story may overwhelm the rest of the sermon. Occasionally, that is the intention, as in a dramatic monologue sermon. More often, the story should be short enough to maintain its force and focus.

Sources for Stories

In some respects, the most difficult aspect of storytelling is finding stories to tell. No less a preacher than Fosdick said that finding good illustrations was the hardest thing he did.[7] Unusual indeed is the person like W. E. Sangster who viewed the craft of sermon illustration as "fun, an occupation of leisure, a recreation with which to reward oneself at the end of a weary day."[8] More commonly, the search for moving stories will leave you weary at the end of the day. The preacher who uses stories regularly soon discovers that his sermons have a voracious appetite for tales to tell. There never seem to be enough. Good stories are rare and precious commodities, seldom the product of labor alone, though not the product of an idle mind either. At best, they are a melding of perception, discipline, and grace.

Discovering External Sources for Stories

Perhaps the least likely place to find good stories is in books of sermon illustrations. Stories from World War I, the Great Depression, Dwight L. Moody, Charles Spurgeon, and the like which are usually found in such "treasure books" seldom connect with contemporary experience. Most people would rather have fresh fish than canned sardines any day. Hence, there are few shortcuts. The places for potential stories are virtually limitless—the Bible, nature, science, art, the media, history, biography, fiction, drama, movies, television, daily events. The repositories are there, but the stories must be lifted out. Unless we are constantly exposed to possible sources, our chances are diminished of discovering those stories which are to be found.

Vast amounts of reading and exposure to different life situations do not guarantee ready-made stories to be told. Stories are happening all around us, but we must recognize and remember them. There is great wisdom in the discipline of systematically recording impressions and events which might lead to stories. Robert McCracken taught his students to live with a notebook into which they regularly transcribed ideas and experiences which might serve as sermon illustrations.[9] The everyday situations of life are pregnant with meaning, but those situations seldom walk up, tap the preacher on the shoulder, and say, "Use me!" Rather, we must learn to see analogically, to notice connections between the visible world and the world of the spirit. The development of depth perception does not happen at once, but as we train our minds to discern metaphorical experiences, the stories do appear.

Fred Craddock offered a proviso about the search for

stories. He warned that a good analogy or illustration can be a pushy, arrogant thing.[10] That entertaining story from the previous week easily finds its way into the sermon on Sunday, whether it belongs there or not. A hallmark of sound preparation is the ability to delay incorporating good stories into sermons until they are needed. Vigilance and perception are not enough. Finding and using good stories also requires restraint.

Developing Internal Sources for Stories

In a sense, all stories are products of the imagination. Here, imagination is not mere fantasizing (though that may be involved), but the capacity to expand our horizons. In order to produce stories, we must risk thinking something new or saying something old in a new way. Like any creative person, the storyteller must be willing to experiment with fresh visions until an authentic image of reality emerges. What distinguishes the preacher from other artists are two things: preachers consciously rely on a transcendent source, and they make Holy Scripture a glass of vision.[11]

Personal experience has a unique and important role in preaching. In some respects, all of the sermon is the product of the preacher's personal experiences. There is an inextricable linkage between the life of the preacher and the content of the sermon. In recent years, that linkage has received new emphasis. The personal reserve of previous generations has sometimes given way to an unapologetic confessionalism in the pulpit.

John Claypool articulated the rational behind confessional preaching, arguing that the only thing we have to share ultimately is ourselves and our experience.[12] He described it as "letting what has happened to you happen through you."[13] Given this intention, it is not only appropriate but necessary that personal incidents be related as stories in sermons. The best help we can offer is our own woundedness and a description of what has saved and healed us. Claypool insisted that this approach was used repeatedly by the apostle Paul. The reason we have three accounts of Paul's conversion in Acts is probably because Paul told his story thousands of times.[14] He allowed what had happened to him to be a means of what might happen through him. Connections are made, rapport is established, trust is engendered, and the gap between pulpit and pew is narrowed when the preacher shares from his own life.

Personal experience may be the most dynamic form of storytelling, but several words of caution are in order. First, personal experiences must not include stories from the preacher's counseling ministry. Even allusions to counseling situations from past places of service will inhibit faith in the pastor's ability to keep matters confidential. People who fear their problems might be turned into sermon illustrations will be reluctant to seek counseling. Second, the overuse of personal incidents in preaching may cause resentment among the congregants. Preachers who constantly talk about themselves in sermons will be seen as egomaniacs or bores. I try not to use more than one personal reference per sermon. Even that may be excessive, depending on how revealing the illustrations are. The preacher who bares his soul every Sunday may find that his audience begins to wince the moment he steps into the pulpit. Personal examples are vital, but they are most effective when they are used cautiously.

The Oral Delivery of Stories

Storytelling is an oral event. Stories in sermons are intended to be spoken, not written. Nevertheless, the way that stories get into speech may be through the vehicle of the written word. David Matthews argued persuasively for the scripting of every part of the sermon. Writers in various disciplines—the media, the theater, politics—write expressly for speaking. On television, virtually every word that is spoken on the air (except for video-taped interviews and talk shows) is first written. Matthews stated that "In such a world of economized language and sophisticated techniques in communication, the even partially extemporaneous preacher is either profoundly gifted or foolish."[15] That is a strong assessment of the need for careful sermon preparation.

Perhaps some preachers are especially gifted and can speak extemporaneously, but most sermons could be improved by scripting, using established guidelines of oral presentations. Some of those principles are as follows:

—Sentences are less involved in structure.
—Fragmentary sentences may be used.
—Slang is acceptable.
—Contractions are used more often.
—A greater amount of repetition is necessary.
—Oral style is more euphonious.
—Concrete words should be used more often.
—The rhythm is different from the rhythm of written style.[16]

Oral style can be enhanced through careful attention to these stylistic techniques. Whether the manuscript is actually taken into the pulpit is another matter. Some, like Claypool and Buttrick, have been able to write out their sermons in full, only to enter the pulpit empty handed and recreate in oral form essentially what they had written. Others tell their sermons/stories from written materials which they have before them. In either case, the meticulous labor of the study bears fruit in the pulpit.

The Use of Pacing and Dramatic Pause

Scripting does not eliminate the need for timing in oral deliveries. With storytelling, timing is even more crucial. Pacing occurs, in part, through the use of pauses. Any storyteller must become comfortable with silence and use it as a means of guiding the attention of the audience. Pauses can signal the beginning of a story, heighten curiosity in the midst of a story, deepen suspense near the climax of a story, and allow time for reflection at the end of a story. Of course, pauses can be too long or used too frequently. However, pauses which are used creatively facilitate the listeners' entry into the story.

Augusta Baker and Ellin Greene have compiled a list of suggestions about timing which are worthy of recording here.

1. Pause before any change of idea, before any significant word.
2. Emphasize words that carry meaning.
3. Imaginative passages should be taken slowly, parts narrating action should be taken rapidly.
4. Change pace as you near the climax.
5. Conversation should be taken at a speed that is appropriate for the character speaking.
6. The pause and the dropped voice can be more effective than the shout.[17]

Obviously, the storyteller who tries to keep all of these principles in mind in the act of telling will have a nervous breakdown. Still, they are helpful as a checklist for reviewing storytelling techniques. Over time, and with practice, these guidelines for pacing can be incorporated into a storyteller's personal style.

The Use of Eye Contact and Gestures

Although storytelling is an oral medium, there is a visual dimension which is equally important. Rare indeed is the preacher who can hold the attention of his audience without looking at them. There is hardly anything so deadly as a sermon which is read word for word from the pulpit. However, Charles Bartow acknowledged that there may be times when indirect eye contact is called for, such as when the preacher wants to focus on mental images or interpersonal moods.[18] Some stories require a certain detachment, a certain pulling back to allow room for the movement of the narrative. Undoubtedly, that is what Fred Craddock had in mind when he said,

> A good storyteller seldom looks at anyone. Some whittle, some look into the glowing fireplace, some never stop walking down the lane, and others lie on the hillside looking at the stars while chewing tender stems of wild grass. They save their eye contact for those occasional didactic turns, when there is a lesson to be planted on the forehead. But stories are always overheard, and in that overhearing there may well be encounter and confrontation.[19]

Thus, eye contact is largely determined by the mood and content of the story. It is ill-advised to look down at the lectern for long stretches of time, but there may be occasions to stare out into space if the tone or a particular movement of the story warrants it.

Gestures are also a vital part of storytelling. Thomas Troeger observed that he remembered some sermons primarily by the gestures that were used, rather than by the words that were spoken.[20] Like pauses, gestures can arrest attention, mark emphasis, and reinforce the mood of what is being told. Kemper divided gestures into two categories: emphatic and descriptive.[21] An emphatic gesture is a kind of visual underlining for emphasis, such as a clenched fist or an extended forefinger. A descriptive gesture helps to portray that image or scene which is being described. Both types of gestures should be natural and spontaneous. Gestures which call attention to themselves may be distracting instead of helpful. Ethel Barrett gave a few rules of thumb. "Don't over-do. Don't become addicted to one gesture. Don't become known for eccentric gestures."[22] These simple guidelines can enable gestures to add interest and support to the telling of the story.

Gestures, facial expressions, posture, and other body language all add shades of meaning and elicit visual feedback from the listeners. Yet technique can become a stumbling block if it inhibits the storyteller's spontaneous involvement in the story. Hence, John Killinger reduced much homiletical theory to three simple suggestions about delivery: preach naturally, preach animatedly, and preach responsively.[23] Stories that come from the heart and are directed in a responsive way towards the congregation will hit their mark. When in harmony with the words that are spoken, gestures and eye contact make the story a language event.

Notes

1. Richard Bandler and John Grindler, *Frogs into Princes: Neuro Linguistic Programming* (Moab, Utah: Real People Press, 1979), pp. iii-iv.
2. William J. Bausch, *Storytelling: Faith and Imagination* (Mystic, Conn.: Twenty-third Publications, 1984), p. 13.
3. James W. Cox, *A Guide to Biblical Preaching* (Nashville: Abingdon, 1976), p. 97.

4. Ian MacPherson, *The Art of Illustrating Sermons* (New York: Abingdon, 1964), p. 163.

5. John Killinger, *Fundamentals of Preaching* (Philadelphia: Fortress Press, 1985), p. 128.

6. George M. Bass, *The Song and the Story* (Lima, Ohio: C.S.S. Publishing Company, 1984), p. 126.

7. Louis W. Bloede, "Preaching and Story," *The Iliff Review,* 37 (Fall 1980), p. 59.

8. W. E. Sangster, *The Craft of Sermon Construction and Illustration* (Grand Rapids: Baker Book House, 1950), p. 16.

9. Charles L. Rice, *Interpretation and Imagination: The Preacher and Contemporary Literature* (Philadelphia: Fortress Press, 1970), p. 103.

10. Fred B. Craddock, *As One Without Authority,* Third ed. (Nashville: Abingdon, 1979), p. 101.

11. Robert D. Young, *Religious Imagination: God's Gift to Prophets and Preachers* (Philadelphia: The Westminster Press, 1979), p. 38.

12. John R. Claypool, *The Preaching Event* (Waco: Word Books, 1980), p. 108.

13. John R. Claypool, "Confessional Preaching," *Preaching in Today's World,* ed. James C. Barry (Nashville: Broadman Press, 1984), p. 59.

14. Ibid., p. 60.

15. C. David Matthews, "Preaching to the Contemporary Mind," *Preaching in Today's World,* ed. James C. Barry (Nashville: Broadman Press, 1984), p. 24.

16. Robert Young, *Be Brief About It* (Philadelphia: The Westminster Press, 1980), p. 87.

17. Augusta Baker and Ellin Greene, *Storytelling: Art & Technique* (New York: R. R. Bowker Company, 1977), p. 46.

18. Charles L. Bartow, *The Preaching Moment: A Guide to Sermon Delivery* (Nashville: Abingdon, 1980), p. 111.

19. Fred B. Craddock, *Overhearing the Gospel* (Nashville: Abingdon, 1978), p. 117.

20. Thomas H. Troeger, *Creating Fresh Images for Preaching* (Valley Forge: Judson Press, 1982), p. 122.

21. Kemper, *Effective Preaching,* p. 127.

22. Ethel Barrett, *Storytelling: It's Easy* (Grand Rapids: Zondervan Publishing House, 1960), pp. 21-22.

23. Killinger, *Fundamentals of Preaching,* pp. 156-159.

5
Using Stories Deductively

Now the eleven disciples went to Galilee, to the mountain to which Jesus had directed them. And when they saw him they worshiped him; but some doubted. And Jesus came and said to them, "All authority in heaven and on earth has been given to me. Go therefore and make disciples of all nations, baptizing them in the name of the Father and of the Son and of the Holy Spirit, teaching them to observe all that I have commanded you; and lo, I am with you always, to the close of the age."

—Matthew 28:16-20

Sermon: But Some Doubted

They say that "seeing is believing." Apparently, that's not always true. I remember the story of a man who was sitting in a theatre watching a movie. After a while he noticed that the woman sitting in front of him had her arm around the neck of a large dog. There they were, sitting side by side, both intently watching the movie. The man could not believe his eyes. The dog obviously understood what was taking place on the screen. He growled at the bad guys, he chuckled under his breath at the funny parts, he even barked during an exciting chase scene. Finally, the man could restrain himself no longer. He leaned forward and tapped the woman on the shoulder

and said, "Pardon me, madam, but I can't believe your
dog's behavior." The woman turned and whispered back.
"Honestly, it amazes me, too. He hated the book." Sometimes it is hard to believe your eyes.

In our Scripture text, we read about another instance
where seeing was not believing. In this passage, Matthew
recorded Jesus' last words to His disciples, Jesus' farewell
address, if you will. It was after the resurrection, and the
eleven disciples had gathered on a mountaintop in Galilee. There Jesus appeared to them and gave them His final
words, words which we now call the Great Commission.
But Matthew included a rather fascinating detail in this
story that we could easily miss. Matthew wrote in verse
17, "When they saw Jesus they worshiped him; but some
doubted." Amazing! After the resurrection, Jesus appeared to the disciples on a mountain in Galilee, but some
doubted. Some of them could not believe their own eyes.
Some of them, even in the presence of the risen Christ,
had doubts about their faith. What an amazing detail for
Matthew to include as a preface for Jesus' last words. And
yet, what a meaningful detail for us today: "But some
doubted."

It was almost thirteen years ago that I entered seminary. To be honest with you, I wasn't sure what to expect.
My vision of the seminary was that it must be a holy place,
filled with holy people. I imagined that everyone there,
including the students, must be some sort of spiritual
giant, that everyone there must have a vast knowledge of
the Bible and a deep faith. And I wasn't sure that I be-
longed in that kind of company. Quite frankly, even entering seminary, I wasn't sure what I believed or why I
believed it. I remember having a great fear that someone
would find out and that I would be expelled from the
seminary as an unbeliever.

Thankfully, I soon discovered that the seminary was not precisely as I had feared. Oh, there were plenty of "preacher boys" running around. There were plenty of aspiring young theologues who exuded a type of piety and who talked the "language of Zion" and who wore their faith on their sleeves. But I also found some fellow students who were like me. I found some fellow honest doubters, some fellow searchers for a faith that could integrate the heart and the mind. And those fellow questers became my support group and my closest friends.

I'm not sure why, but somewhere along the line we got the idea that doubt is a bad thing. Somewhere we got the notion that doubts are something to be ashamed of, that doubts are weak, sinful, and pagan. I, like most of you, have heard sermons condemning doubts and placing loads of guilt on those of us with spiritual uncertainties. When I first got to seminary, I was afraid to admit my doubts because I thought that doubts were unacceptable. *But this passage in Matthew puts the issue of religious doubts in an entirely different light.*

Above all, this passage teaches us something about the nature of faith. Throughout the Gospels, Jesus made it plain that seeing is not necessarily believing. There were plenty of people who saw Jesus do marvelous things, yet did not believe. And Jesus did not try to prove Himself to them. Jesus did not try to convince people by miracles or by rationale arguments that He was the Messiah. I imagine that Jesus could have won more than His share of debates, but Jesus knew that arguments do not lead to faith. Jesus could have dazzled them with His powers, but He knew that was not the way to faith either. No, Jesus did not, would not, coerce people into believing. Faith was, and always will be, a matter of individual choice. Doubt is inevitable. Someone has said that "doubt is the vestibule of faith." Doubt is the shadow side of faith. That means that if people are really free to believe, they must also be free to doubt.

I'm not sure I can explain why some of those disciples on the mountaintop still had doubts about Jesus. You would think by then, when they saw Jesus risen from the dead, that they could not help but believe. But apparently, some of them did not. At least they had their doubts. And that may be simply a part of the nature of faith. Some level of doubt may be normal. Certainly, not all of us are in the same place in terms of our religious faith. Certainly, God does not expect us to have the same level of religious belief. If we are truly free to believe, then we will probably believe to different extents.

What I am trying to say is that doubts, in and of themselves, are neither good nor bad—they are simply inevitable. Doubts are a natural human reaction to that which is new or mysterious. The poet and philosopher Samuel Taylor Coleridge once said, "Never be afraid of doubt, if only you have the disposition to believe." There is a lot of truth in those words. "Never be afraid of doubt, if only you have the disposition to believe." *It is the presence or absence of that disposition to believe which determines whether doubts are positive or negative.* In other words, without a willingness to believe, doubts can be destructive. Without a willingness to believe, doubts can give way to cynicism, despondency, or despair. Yes, doubts can be harmful but only when we allow them to have the final word.

I recall some advice that the dean at the seminary gave us entering students. He warned us that during the course of our studies, our immature faith would be challenged. As we learned more and more about the Bible and Christian history, our minds would be stretched. As we thought

more deeply about God, our belief structure might very
well be threatened. After all, there is a lot in the Bible
they don't teach you in Sunday School. When it comes to
trying to reconcile the different stories in the Gospels or
to understand "holy war" in the Old Testament, it can get
rather confusing. And there is a lot about church politics
that can be disillusioning. But the dean cautioned us not
to be hasty about giving up our old beliefs. He said, "Don't
leave what you have until you find something better."
Don't put away your childhood faith until you develop a
more mature faith. In other words, make sure you step
onto solid land before you step out of the boat. Yes, doubts
can be destructive if we allow them to overwhelm our
faith. But there can be a positive side to doubts as well.
Doubts can be the gateway to a greater faith. As Tennyson
said,

> There lives more faith in honest doubt,
> Believe me, than in half the creeds.

Doubts can nudge us on to a more mature faith. Doubts
can help us to put aside inadequate ideas about God or
Christ or the Christian life or the church. Doubts can help
us to challenge traditional wisdom which may not be so
wise at all. As Frederick Buechner said, "Doubts are the
ants in the pants of faith; doubts keep faith awake and
moving."

Religious certainty, carried to its logical extreme, has
always been a dangerous thing. A religion without doubts
can easily lead to fanaticism. We see the results of Moslem
fanaticism in countries like Iran and Iraq. We see religious
fanaticism in Northern Ireland, India, or even among
cults in our own country. Those religions which allow no
doubts, which claim to have a "corner on the market" of

truth, can be a dangerous menace. Christianity is not immune to this malady.

Yes, doubts can be very positive if doubts help us to recognize that no mortal fully possesses the ultimate truth. Doubts can help us to see that we are finite, limited, that we do not have all the answers. Doubts can shake our arrogance and temper our pride. Doubts can open us to receive more truth, if only we have the disposition to believe.

How then do we deal with our doubts in a constructive way? Our Scripture text provides the clue. I find it fascinating that Jesus did not try to answer their doubts. Jesus did not try to convince those doubting disciples to believe. Jesus did not try to prove to them that He really was alive. Jesus did not give them a single argument to assuage their unbelief. No, Jesus gave them something better. He gave them a job to do and people to do it with. It was as if Jesus were saying, "The church and My work are the answer to your doubts. Be about My business, and your doubts will take care of themselves."

George Matheson was a Scottish preacher, poet, and pastor of a century ago. He wrote the famous hymn, "O Love That Wilt Not Let Me Go." But in his early years, while he was a pastor in the Scottish highlands, Matheson had a crisis of faith. He began to be plagued by doubts, so that he could no longer believe in God the way he once did. Finally, he decided that to remain true to his conscience, he must resign from his church and leave the ministry. But his church would not let him go. They told him to stay and to preach as much about Christianity as he could believe in. So he stayed. Gradually, as he pastored that church, he was able to deal with his doubts and to grow beyond them. Gradually, Matheson discovered that the answer to doubts is not some convincing argument but life with God's people, doing God's work. Gradually, it was faith, not doubts, which had the final say in his life until he could write the words to that beautiful hymn:

> O love that wilt not let me go,
> I rest my weary soul in thee;
> I give thee back the life I owe,
> That in thine ocean depths its flow
> May richer, fuller be.

What happened to George Matheson has been my experience as well. I do not claim to have all the answers now, but I am no longer hounded by doubts as I once was. Perhaps as I have become more involved in the life and work of the church, my own faith has grown. But I do not take that faith for granted, nor should you take your faith for granted. Each day, each stage of life, brings its own challenges and questions. I suppose I will always have doubts, or at least questions, about some things. But of this I am certain, doubts need not have the final word.

Just as Jesus met George Matheson and those doubting disciples, so Jesus meets you and me in our doubting. He does not give us a set of convincing arguments, only a convincing Person. He does not guarantee answers to all of our questions; He only guarantees He will be with us. "Lo, I am with you always," He said (Matt. 28:20). Somehow, that is enough.

Stories That Were Told

This sermon contains a number of stories or story fragments. First, the sermon is based on a biblical story, namely the account of Jesus giving the Great Commission from a mountaintop in Galilee. This is the major narrative of the sermon, and it is alluded to throughout. A second story opens the sermon proper. It is an amusing anecdote about a woman and a dog watching a movie. A true-life story follows from my own experience, the story about my religious doubts and fears of being discovered upon entering seminary. A related story is the advice which the seminary dean gave us as entering students. Later, there are various story fragments in the allusions to religious fanaticism around the world. Since the news has been full of such incidents, these allusions probably conjure up various stories in the minds of the listeners. The final story in the sermon is the way George Matheson dealt with his doubts. Thus, stories comprise a major portion of the sermon and are used during each movement of the sermon to make concrete that which is proposed.

Analysis

Virtually all of the stories in this sermon are used deductively as examples. In almost every case, a propositional statement is made and then supported by an example story. The sermon begins with the statement, "Seeing is not necessarily believing." The story of the woman and the dog in the movie provides an example of that proposition. The biblical story is then related to further exemplify the veracity of that opening statement.

The personal story about my own doubts upon entering seminary is used to support the contention that doubting is normal. Through that real-life example, people are shown that doubts are natural, not an aberration. Because the story is somewhat confessional, people are invited to identify with the preacher and are given the license to acknowledge their own doubts. Thus, this story is crucial to engender the trust necessary for the rest of the sermon to be convincing.

The related story about the seminary dean's advice demonstrates the negative side of doubt. From the story, it becomes apparent that there is a danger in allowing doubts to dislodge us from our previous beliefs until we are ready to move on to a more mature faith. Although this story is very brief, almost a mere quotation, it does continue the antecedent story about my own personal doubts.

The final proposition that doubts can be dealt with in a positive way is substantiated by two stories: the biblical story and the story about George Matheson. The biblical story demonstrates how Jesus deals with our doubts, not by giving us arguments or signs but by giving us a commission. The George Matheson story reinforces this assertion by providing an actual incident where doubt was overcome by involvement in Christ's work. Because it is also related to a beloved hymn "O Love That Wilt Not Let Me Go," the emotional appeal of the story is enhanced.

Without these stories, the sermon could be reduced to a series of didactic assertions:

—seeing is not necessarily believing;
—doubt is a normal human function;
—doubts can have a negative side;
—doubts also can have a positive dimension;
—Jesus can deal with our doubts in a constructive way.

The sermon could be so reduced, but at a considerable loss. However, by using stories deductively as examples, each assertion was supported, deepened, personalized, and actualized. With the stories, the sermon could be more accurately outlined as follows:

—seeing is not necessarily believing;
    anecdote about woman and dog at the movie, bibli-

cal story about doubting disciples on the mountaintop;
—doubt is a normal human function;
   story of the preacher's doubts upon entering seminary;
—doubts can have a negative side;
   seminary professor's advice;
—doubts can have a positive dimension;
   examples of fanaticism in religions without doubts;
—Jesus can deal with our doubts in a constructive way;
   biblical story, with focus on Great Commission; account of George Matheson's doubt and the outcome.

In various ways, the smaller stories serve as commentary on the larger biblical story and as bridges to the
individual stories of the listeners. They provide specific
examples to support the logical statements and aid in the
movement of the sermon toward its conclusion. Thus,
through the deductive use of stories as examples, the basic
ideas of the sermon are exemplified, deepened, and made
relevant to the situation of the listeners.

6
Using Stories
Inductively as Illustrations

Praise the Lord, O my soul;
  all my inmost being, praise his holy name.
Praise the Lord, O my soul,
  and forget not all his benefits.
He forgives all my sins
  and heals all my diseases;
he redeems my life from the pit
  and crowns me with love and compassion.
He satisfies my desires with good things,
  so that my youth is renewed like the eagle's.
The Lord works righteousness
  and justice for all the oppressed.
He made known his ways to Moses,
  his deeds to the people of Israel:
The Lord is compassionate and gracious,
  slow to anger, abounding in love.
                    —Psalm 103:1-8 (NIV)

Sermon: Who'll Stop the Rain?

Psalm 103 is one of the most beautiful passages of Scripture in all the Bible. Perhaps you are more familiar with the King James Version of Psalm 103:1-4:

Bless the Lord, O my soul; and all that is within me, bless his holy name. Bless the Lord, O my soul, and forget not all his benefits: Who forgiveth all thine iniquities, who

healeth all thy diseases; Who redeemeth thy life ʿrom de-
struction; who crowneth thee with lovingkindness and
tender mercies; ... Bless the Lord, O my soul: and all that
is within me, bless his holy name (v. 1, repeated).

It is a beautiful thought. God loves us. God has compassion for us. God showers us with blessings. God is merciful
to us. God will not hold a grudge against us. God forgives
our sins. God heals our diseases. God delivers us from
illness and death. God is on our side. God wants the best
for us. God will take care of us. It is a beautiful thought.
But is it true?

Item: Albion, Pennsylvania. One afternoon recently a
tornado touched down in that tiny town and wreaked a
terrible toll. Sandra Stahlsmith and her two children, ages
six and nine, took refuge in the basement of their home.
The twister hit, and the walls of the house caved in upon
them. Mrs. Stahlsmith told what happened next. "I felt
my little boy being crushed," she said. "He took two
breaths, and I knew he was dead. He died in my arms. I'll
never sleep again." Altogether, over ninety other people
died, hundreds were injured, and thousands lost their
homes across three states and a province in Canada.

Item: The Ganges Delta of Bangladesh. Only days
before the tornadoes in the Northeast, a deadly cyclone
and tidal wave swept away at least ten thousand souls. The
latest count: two-hundred thousand homes destroyed;
one-hundred-thirty-five thousand acres of cropland
ruined; untold hundreds of thousands of people suffering
injury, disease, shock, hunger, and grief.

Item: The sub-Sahara of Africa. A drought threatens the
future of a whole generation. Two million people have
already died. Millions more, three quarters of them chil-

dren, are in imminent danger of death from starvation or the ghastly diseases associated with famine.

Item: Annapolis, Maryland. A young mother waged a long and difficult battle with painful cancer. The disease finally prevailed, and the woman died at age thirty-seven. She left behind a grieving husband and two children. Item: another heartache, another tragedy, another death; you fill in the details. And our spirits cry out: How do you reconcile the love of God with that?

Psalm 103 is a beautiful statement about God's love, mercy, compassion, and pity. It is a beautiful sentiment, but in the face of all the senseless suffering around us in our world, our spirits cry out, "Can it possibly be true?" If God really loves us, why all the pain? If God really watches over us, why is there a twister over Albion, a wall of water from the Bay of Bengal, a drought which lasts for years, or diseases which ravage young people in the prime of life? Our spirits cry out, "Why?" If God is on our side, if God is for us, if God is with us, why? There is no more difficult question for the Christian faith.

The English philosopher John Hick wrote a massive four-hundred page study entitled *Evil and the God of Love*. Hick began the book with these words: "The fact of evil constitutes the most serious objection there is to the Christian belief in a God of love." And for the next four-hundred pages, Hick tries to explain how it is possible to still believe in a loving God. It is a difficult challenge. If anything can cause us to doubt God's goodness, it is the senseless tragedy and innocent suffering that happens around us.

This is not just some philosophical exercise, you see. This is not just some hypothetical, abstract, theological discussion. It's happening all around us. Maybe it has already happened in your own life. Natural evil, misfortune, bad luck, tragic events, terrible incurable diseases, floods and fires, tornadoes and hurricanes, and earthquakes and all manner of what the insurance companies call "acts of God." It's happening all around us, and our spirits cry out, "Why?" We read Psalm 103 about the love of God, and we look at our world, and our spirits cry out, "Why?" How do we reconcile the love of God with the tragedies of life?

Please notice that up to this point I have been very careful to talk about a specific kind of evil—natural evil. I have not mentioned tragedies which are the result of human sin. I have not talked about the thirty-eight people who were stomped to death in a soccer game in Brussels. I have not talked about the scores of people who die from drug overdoses every year on the streets of Washington. I have not talked about the innocent victims of crime. I have not talked about those who perish in traffic accidents at the hands of drunken drivers. I have not talked about the victims of the Nazi Holocaust or the more recent holocaust in Cambodia. I have not talked about those who have died in wars or in airplane crashes. Yes, these are very real tragedies, too, but they are tragedies produced by human error or human sin. It is obvious that God is not responsible for murder, drug abuse, or traffic accidents. The gift of human freedom carries with it the potential to misuse that freedom to hurt others or to hurt ourselves. No, tragedies caused by human error and human sin cannot be blamed on God. But natural evil—disease and drought and other terrible acts of nature—natural evil is much more difficult to understand. Natural evil raises disturbing questions. Does God really love us, and if He really does love us, then why does He allow so much suffering and pain?

Woody Allen had a line in one of his movies which

reflected these difficult questions. In the movie *Love and Death*, the Woody Allen character said at one point, "If it turns out there is a God, I don't think He's evil—the best thing you can say about Him is that He's an underachiever." Judging by recent events—the tornadoes, the tidal wave, the drought, fatal diseases—it might appear that Woody Allen is right. It does sometimes appear that God is an underachiever, that God has not quite lived up to expectations. Judging by recent events, when bad things happen to good people, it is easy to question God's love. That's why Psalm 103 is so important for us today. Psalm 103 is important because it affirms that God does love us, that God does want the best for us. And the way things are going, we need that kind of reminder.

Psalm 103 is especially important when we place it in the context of all the other psalms. The Book of Psalms is not some naive "pie in the sky," "rose-colored glasses," everything-is-hunky-dory bedtime story. No, taken together, the Psalms recognize that life is a hard road, full of hardships, hard times, and hard knocks. In over half of the Psalms, the writer was in distress, the writer was crying out to God for help. Martin Marty said the context of many of the Psalms is the "wintry landscape of the heart". By that he meant that many of the Psalms were written amidst the crisis of life, the difficult circumstances of life, the terrible times of loneliness, suffering, doubt, grief, and despair. Taken together, the Psalms acknowledge that life is often interrupted by heartache, yet the psalmist said, "Bless the Lord, O my soul: and all that is within me, bless his holy name." How is that possible? How can we have faith in the love of God when things go so wrong? The key is the psalmist's understanding of life.

Notice toward the end of Psalm 103 the way that the psalmist described life upon this earth. It is like grass, he

said. Our lives are like the wild flowers that bloom on the
hillside. Sooner or later the wind will come, and we will
be gone. God did not make us to live forever upon this
earth. Does that make life any less valuable? On the con-
trary, knowing that our days are numbered makes the
time we have all the more precious. But there is a deeper
truth here. Because our days pass so quickly, it matters
what we do with the time that God has given us.

A couple of months ago, we had a yard sale here at the
church, and I'll admit I looked over the merchandise
before the sale officially began. I was working in my office
when two of our members began to bring in their treasures for the sale, and I couldn't help but notice two red
skateboards with handles on them. Of course, I had to try
them out to make sure they worked, so I made a few runs
up and down the hallway. A little later in the afternoon
my son Marc came by the church, and the skateboards
immediately caught his eye, too. Well, one thing led to
another, and eventually those skateboards ended up in
my garage—one for Marc and one for Amy.

There was great excitement around our house that
night as both kids anticipated using those skateboards on
the sidewalks in our neighborhood. The next day, early in
the morning, Marc and Amy were out racing those skateboards up and down the sidewalk in front of our house. It
wasn't long before Marc came crying into the house with
a skinned knee. His mother put a bandage on it and out
he went, but it was only a matter of minutes before he
came back into the house with the other knee skinned,
too. Hardly a day later, Amy took a terrible fall off her
skateboard, skinning both knees, both hands, an elbow,
and a shoulder. It was all I could do to keep my wife from
throwing those skateboards in the trash. But we still have

them, and the kids still ride them, and the accidents have lessened as the days have gone by.

I realize there was a risk in giving my kids those skateboards in the first place. Oh, I suppose I could have walked alongside them and held their hands and tried to protect them from falling whenever they went out to ride. But after a while, skateboarding wouldn't be any fun any more. There wouldn't be any challenge to it, there wouldn't be any point to it if the father was always hanging on.

Yes, there was risk, and there was some pain, but that's the way we and our world are made. If there were no risk in life, things would be rather boring. If there were no challenges, life would be like a game where you always win. If there were no need to learn new skills, solve difficult problems, or develop our potential, life would be pointless indeed. If this earth were some perfectly safe paradise, with no work to be done, no responsibilities to be borne, no obstacles to be overcome, it would be a mind-dulling, monotonous existence. But God took the risk of giving us skateboards. God took the risk of creating a world where things are not always safe. God took the risk in creating a world where there is work to be done. God took the risk in placing us in an environment full of challenges and opportunities, and even threats, because that is the only kind of world in which we can truly grow.

It is precisely because God does love us that He placed us in this kind of world. And it is precisely because God loves us that He gives us the freedom to ride our skateboards, and yes, even the freedom to fall. I suppose God could hold our hands and walk alongside of us and protect us from every ill wind or storm that blows. I suppose God could calm every hurricane and seed every cloud over a drought-stricken land and wipe out every disease; I suppose God could do all that, but then, life would be without a goal. If our world were a perfect paradise, we would never know the joy of discovery; we would never know the satisfaction of helping someone in need; we would never know the meaning of compassion or the cost of love or the need for faith. I suppose God could have given us a perfect world where everything is already done, but, then, there would be nothing left for us to do.

I don't remember where I read it, but there was a wonderful letter to the editor in a recent newspaper or magazine about the terrible famine in Africa. The writer said, "I used to scream at God about all the starving children until I realized that the starving children were God screaming at me".

I don't know if the day will ever come when all the natural evils of this world are overcome, but I do know that God has placed us on this earth to work toward that day. I don't know if we will ever be able to solve the problem of drought and famine, but I do know that God has placed us on the earth to try to solve those problems. I don't know if we will ever conquer dreaded diseases like cancer, heart ailments, and genetic disorders, but I do know that God has given us minds to think and hearts to care for those who suffer. I don't know if we will ever eliminate those senseless tragedies like tornadoes, cyclones, earthquakes, and tidal waves, but I do know there is much we can do right now to make the world a better place in which to live. I don't know that we can ever make the world a perfect place, but I do know that God will work to perfect us if only we will let him. I don't know that we will ever make sense out of all the suffering and tragedy and pain in life, but I do know that God loves us in the suffering, in the tragedy, and in the pain, and somehow that does make a difference.

One final thing. When Marc and Amy came crying into our house with skinned knees and elbows and hands, Linda did not say, "There, there, don't cry, it doesn't matter; they will eventually heal." No, their mother took them in her arms, and she wiped away their tears, and she held them until there was no reason to cry anymore. Yes, the wounds will eventually heal, but the crying does matter, the hurt does matter. You can be sure that God has His arms around a lot of folks. And you can be sure that when you get hurt, God will put His arms around you too. "Bless the Lord, O my soul: and all that is within me, bless his holy name."

Stories that Were Told

After some opening observations about the Scripture text, the sermon launches into four brief stories about public and private tragedies. The first three have been in the news: tornadoes in Pennsylvania, a cyclone in Bangladesh, and drought/famine in Africa. The stories are related with little embellishment but with enough detail to provide some emotional impact. A fourth ministory, about the cancer death of a young woman in Annapolis, Maryland, personalizes the tragedies. The young woman who died of cancer is known to many members of the congregation. Some actively ministered to her during her final days of illness. Hence, the philosophical questions raised by John Hick's book have a deeply experiential reference in the minds of many of the listeners. They witnessed a young woman of genuine faith in a loving God suffer an agonizing death.

The sermon continues with a number of brief references to tragic incidents which are not the results of natural evil. Such events as people dying from a mob stampede at a soccer game, drug overdoses, drunk driving, and evil political regimes are mentioned, almost in passing. These references lack most of the characteristics of narrative, but they do conjure up recollections of stories in the news about which the listeners are probably familiar.

The final story is the major contemporary narrative in the sermon. With some detail and a touch of humor, I describe the discovery and the purchase of skateboards for my children, as well as the consequent accidents involving the use of those skateboards. This story and its subsequent analogical applications, address the major theological issues raised by the preceding stories and comprise almost one quarter of the entire sermon.

Analysis

Although no sermon fits any category perfectly, there are definite inductive movements in this sermon, particularly with regard to the stories. The initial quartet of stories moves from specific instances of tragedy to the more general question: How do we reconcile God's love with innocent suffering? Hence, those four brief stories are used as illustrations to challenge the ebullient tone of the opening paragraphs of the introduction. The stories move the sermon to tension, conflict, and disequilibrium. Rather than using a propositional statement to flatly challenge the opening assertions about the goodness of God, the sermon introduces these four stories to allow the listener to be drawn into the issue and thereby discover the conundrum of natural evil.

The story about the young cancer victim known to the congregation serves to crystallize the theodicy question as well as to personalize the pain of innocent suffering. Not only is the issue a philosophical dilemma for the congregation, but because it was one of their own who died of

cancer, it has become a personal crisis of faith. It illus-
trates that none of us is immune from the problem. Even
deeply religious persons are not protected from the quan-
dry.

The movement of the sermon is facilitated not just by
the stories but also by a number of quotations. There is a
quote from John Hick and a somewhat humorous line
from Woody Allen about the problem of evil. In addition,
there is a quotation from a letter to the editor which shifts
the focus to our responsibility to respond to innocent suffering. These quotations work together with the stories to
enhance the movement of the sermon.

The last story is the major analogical device of the sermon. A number of comparisons are drawn between the
story of the skateboards and the relationship of God to our
world. The role of the parents in the skateboard story
functions as a metaphor for God's behavior toward us. The
story is used to point to the truth that risk is a part of God's
design for human life, for it is only in this kind of environment that we can truly grow. This story is also used at the
end of the sermon to point to the compassion of God in
the face of suffering. Thus, at several points, the story is
used analogically to address the major question of the
sermon and to provide some kind of resolution.

These stories illustrate how stories can be used inductively to analogically point to sermonic truth. Without
them, there would be little from the Scripture text itself
to arouse interest, introduce tension, or provide disequilibrium. In short, without the stories in this sermon, there
were be no sermon. We could read the Scripture text,
with which almost everyone present would agree, and
then go home. But the stories challenge the text and thus
push the listeners to a deeper level of understanding. The
net result is an affirmation of the text, but an affirmation

borne of struggle with the theodicy question. Since the stories were used inductively, the listeners are allowed to experience the conflict for themselves and in their own minds to seek some resolution. Through this inductive process, the Scripture text can finally speak even more forcefully to the concrete situation of the hearers.

7
Using Stories
as Controlling Metaphors

But a man named Ananias with his wife Sapphira sold
a piece of property, and with his wife's knowledge he kept
back some of the proceeds, and brought only a part of it
and laid it at the apostles' feet. But Peter said, "Ananias,
why has Satan filled your heart to lie to the Holy Spirit and
to keep back part of the proceeds of the land? While it
remained unsold, did it not remain your own? And after
it was sold, was it not at your disposal? How is it that you
have contrived this deed in your heart? You have not lied
to men but to God." When Ananias heard these words, he
fell down and died. . . .

After an interval of about three hours his wife came in,
not knowing what had happened. And Peter said to her,
"Tell me whether you sold the land for so much." And she
said, "Yes, for so much." But Peter said to her, "How is it
that you have agreed together to tempt the Spirit of the
Lord? Hark, the feet of those that have buried your husband are at the door, and they will carry you out." Immediately she fell down at his feet and died. When the young
man came in they found her dead, and they carried her
out and buried her beside her husband. And great fear
came upon the whole church, and upon all who heard of
these things (Acts 5:1-11).

Sermon: Lies, Flies, and Alibis

I know hospitals. I've probably been in more hospitals around here than most doctors. As a minister, I have visited people in at least twenty different hospitals here in the metropolitan area. I've been in Walter Reed, in Bethesda Naval, in NIH, in Johns Hopkins, in two of the Adventist hospitals, in Suburban, Sibley, Providence, Doctors, Holy Cross, you name it. But the one hospital which really galls me when I visit is _____ General. Oh, it has nothing to do with the quality of care—I'm sure it's excellent. It has nothing to do with the facilities—the building is quite new and thoroughly modern. It has nothing to do with the location—I can get there easily enough.

No, what really galls me is the parking. There is virtually no place for the visitor to legally park except in the paid parking garage. And you know how we ministers are. If there is a way to avoid paying for parking, we'll find it. I'll walk several blocks if I can park for free. But at _____ General, you have no choice. You have to park in the garage, and whether you stay a few minutes or a few months, you have to pay the same fee to exit—$1.50. What's more, you pay with a token. You have to purchase a token from a machine inside the hospital lobby and then insert the token into a toll gate before leaving the parking garage. And if you have no money, or forget your token, you cannot get out, you're trapped inside forever—or so I thought.

Several weeks ago I was over to visit _____ at _____ General Hospital. I was very careful to purchase my token in the lobby and to have it in hand in the parking garage when I was ready to leave. The token is about the size of a quarter, so you have to be careful not to drop it or lose it before you put it in the tollgate. I was concentrating on hanging on to my token as I pulled up behind a little red Volkswagen just ahead of me at the tollgate. The Volkswagen was behind another car about to exit from the parking garage. The first driver put his token in the box, the gate went up, and he drove his car through. But before the gate could come down, the driver in the little red Volkswagen gunned his engine and pulled right on through behind the first car. He had figured out a way to beat the system. Either he was a very quick thinker, or he had been planning all along to scoot out of the parking garage behind another car without paying the fee. In either case, I was dumbfounded. It never even occurred to me to try to get out without paying. I was so concentrating on paying my token at the proper time, I was left with my mouth hanging open. Yet it struck me, even then, that what that driver did can be a parable of life.

If Ananias and Sapphira were alive today, they would be the kind of people who would try to exit from the parking garage without paying. They would be the kind of people who are always looking for a way to beat the system. They would think nothing about cheating the hospital out of a $1.50 parking fee. After all, they thought nothing about cheating the church, or even cheating God.

When you think about it, it is remarkable that we even have the story of Ananias and Sapphira. It is remarkable that Luke recorded this rather negative event. But he did, so we know that from the very beginning, the church has had its share of liars, hypocrites, and frauds. Black sheep are nothing new to the church. There were some bad apples in the Christian community from the very start.

There were some poor people in that first church in Jerusalem, and in order to care for the needy, some members sold their property and gave the proceeds to the apostles for distribution. Of course, such acts of generosity did not go unnoticed. (If someone were to sell a house and give the money to *this* church, you can be sure we would notice that.) Ananias and Sapphira also noticed, and they wanted some of that acclaim and admiration for themselves. So Ananias and Sapphira, of their own free wills, also sold a piece of property. But instead of giving all the money to the church, the pocketed a portion of the proceeds for themselves and then acted as if they were turning over all of the profit to the apostles. They had figured out a way to beat the system, they thought. They could have their cake and eat it too. They could enjoy the spotlight and still have a little nest egg left over. They thought they could lie to the church and to God and get away with it. But it didn't work. Their lies found them out. First Ananias, and then Sapphira, were confronted with their deception, and they dropped dead right on the spot.

What exactly happened to Ananias and Sapphira? To be honest, we cannot say for sure. Perhaps they were so shocked and humiliated that they suffered heart attacks. Perhaps their sense of guilt was so great that they simply gave up living. Luke implied that their deaths were in some way God's judgment. The popular view that I learned as a child when I first heard this story is that God zapped them for lying. It is a chilling thought.

Recently our family has begun to eat some of our meals outside on the deck in our backyard. We had heard about the problem of bugs and mosquitoes and other flying varmints in some parts of Bowie, so we invested in one of those electronic "bug zappers" to keep from being eaten ourselves. Those "bug zappers" are really quite ingenious. It's basically a bright light bulb surrounded by an electrified coil. As the bugs fly close to the light, they get zapped by the wire. As darkness descends, you begin to hear . . . buzz, zap . . . buzz, zap . . . each time accompanied by a tiny flash of light and a puff of smoke.

Now I'm not suggesting that is what happened to Ananias and Sapphira. If God zapped them for lying, why hasn't God zapped all the other liars, cheats, and frauds? No, it is too simple to conclude that God struck them dead because they cheated. Above all, ours is a faith which affirms the mercy of God. We believe that God will forgive us our sins and help us to live better lives. But the mercy of God does not eradicate the natural consequences of wrong behavior. Certain actions bring with them their own penalties. You cannot jump out the window of a tall building and not suffer the consequences. You cannot step out into the street in front of a speeding automobile and not feel the results of your actions. And, as the Bible would tell us, you cannot lie to God, cheat other people, and get away with it. Sooner or later, the toll must be paid.

There is a caution, then, in this story about seeking the spotlight. Ananias and Sapphira wanted the praise of their fellow church members. They wanted esteem, recognition, and credit for their magnanimity. They wanted center stage, so they made a big display of their so-called sacrifice. But imagine their shock when Peter called their bluff. They probably thought Peter was going to congratulate them for all they had done. Instead, Peter called them liars to their faces. They had sought the glory of the spotlight, but when the light did shine down upon them, it only revealed their shame. There is a danger in seeking to exalt ourselves, to make a name for ourselves, and to glorify ourselves. Perhaps we should remember what happens to the bugs who fly too near the light in my backyard. We can bring incredible pain upon ourselves by seeking the spotlight. God doesn't have to zap us. The natural consequences of selfish behavior are punishment in themselves.

There is a second lesson in this story—a lesson about ethics and morality. It does matter what kind of persons we are. It does matter whether we are persons of honesty and integrity or whether we are always trying to beat the system. In our society, the modern credo seems to be, "Anything goes, as long as you don't get caught." Anything is OK, as long as we can get away with it. If America is on the decline, it is not an economic, political, or military decline; it is a moral decline. George Gallup, the pollster, reports that the United States is one of the most crime-ridden countries in the world. One person in five will be mugged, robbed, assaulted, or have their house broken into this year. There are so many criminals, we cannot build enough prisons to hold them. But it's not just the "criminals." If the recent news is any indication, ethics have gone awry in the business world, too.

In the last few weeks, at least three major corporations have admitted illegal practices. If the recent news is any indication, fraud, cheating, price fixing, inside stock trading, price gouging are common in the marketplace. And it's not just corruption in the big corporations. Department stores lose about $4 billion annually to stealing. The Internal Revenue Service claims that it loses $100 billion a year to income-tax cheating. And on it goes. Cheating in marriages is commonplace. Chances are you know someone right now who is engaged in an extramarital affair. Or you know about dishonesty where you work. Again, George Gallup notes the irony. While religious belief seems to be on the rise in America today, personal morality is on the decline. Almost anything goes. Scoot under the tollgate if you can. Beat the system, do whatever it takes to get ahead, only don't get caught.

Somehow, we have lost the message that personal morality is important. Honesty, integrity, telling the truth, and fidelity are important. I would not point any fingers, but Ananias and Sapphira are with us still. And sadly, they are with us, not just in the business world, not just in the marketplace, not just in the neighborhood, not just in the classroom; but, sadly, Ananaias and Sapphira are with us even in the church.

It was bad enough that Ananias and Sapphira tried to deceive the apostles, but worse yet, they tried to lie to God. They tried to cheat on their religion. They tried to get away with halfhearted commitment. In some ways, hypocrisy may be the worst sin of all.

Hypocrisy may be the worst sin because hypocrisy is basically a willing disobedience. The hypocrite knows better, but he tries to get away with it anyway. The hypocrite knows how God wants him to live, but he thinks he's figured out a way to fool God and beat the system. Sadly, there is a bit of Ananias and Sapphira in all of us, for hypocrisy and halfhearted commitment all too often creep into our lives as well. It's not that we consciously try to cheat God. But oh, how tempting it is to hold something back: our money, our time, our talents, our energies, our enthusiasm, our helpfulness, our willingness to serve. Oh, how easy it is to hoard God's gifts, all the while pretending that we are giving Him our all.

Jesus made it plain. God doesn't want our money; He doesn't want our time; He doesn't want our volunteer services. He wants *us*. If it were just the money God was after, Ananias and Sapphira would have fared pretty well. After all, they did give something, but they did not give themselves. They held back that which is most important, and they died. Ashamed, embarrassed, humiliated, without honor, devoid of dignity, alone—they died. Like bugs on a grid, their lives were ended in a flash, and all that we remember about them is their shame.

I suppose there will always be an Ananias and Sapphira. There will always be those who try to slip through the toll-gates of life without paying their dues. There will always be those who seek only the spotlight, who lie if they have to and cheat if they can. There will always be those who play games at religion, who offer God only a portion and keep the best for themselves. There will always be those who try to fool their neighbors and even fool God, but in the end, they will have only fooled themselves.

The way of honesty is seldom the easy way. The way of self-giving and self-sacrifice is often costly. But God should know. On a lonely hill called Calvary He held nothing back for us. He gave Himself for our sakes, as much as He could give. Strange as it may seem, the tollgate to life, and life eternal, is a cross. And in a way that we will never fully understand, God has already paid the toll and set us free. There is no reason to hold anything back, you see. We already have it all. There is no reason for lying, no reason for deceit, no reason for hypocrisy. God has given us Himself. And that, in our heart of hearts, is all we shall ever want or ever really need.

Stories that Were Told

Two major stories dominate this sermon: the biblical story about Ananias and Sapphira and the story about the cheater at the hospital parking garage tollgate. The biblical story is, of course, the more memorable and powerful, but the hospital story does serve as something of a modern-day equivalent. Although I did not make it explicit, I have a hunch that the Ananias and Sapphira story has many built-in connections with people living in affluent, modern suburbia. The real-estate theme is important—

after all, many people move into suburban areas because of affordable real estate and for investment purposes. Also, the concern which Ananias and Sapphira had for social standing and "keeping up with the Joneses" is a suburban theme. Thus, the biblical story has many hooks for snagging upper-middle-class, suburban church people.

A lesser story, though still important, is the account of our backyard barbeque with the bug problem. It provides a ready point of identification as well as a somewhat humorous, somewhat serious metaphor: the big zapper. Although the brief incident was told almost as an aside, allusions to it occur at several points throughout the rest of the sermon. Thus, this minor story also serves a function. It uses a touch of humor to connect with the plight of the characters in the biblical story, but also to connect with the consequences of sin in our lives.

Other narrative material includes statistics and quotations from the Gallup Survey organization and a few story fragments. Recent news reports about corporate corruption are mentioned, though few details are given. It is assumed that most people are aware of revelations about the latest big-business scandals, so they are related in passing. Still, those references serve in a minor way to support the contention that there is the danger of moral decline in American culture.

Analysis

The major contemporary story about the hospital parking-lot fraud provides the major metaphor for the sermon: the tollgate. This metaphor is used in a number of ways, virtually from the beginning to the end of the sermon. First, the tollgate deception is used to describe the behavior of Ananias and Sapphira. The action of the offender at the tollgate provides an equivalent for the kind of attitude evidenced by Ananias and Sapphira. The metaphor of the tollgate makes their offense contemporary. Their deceit was not just a product of their times. That same temptation to take advantage of the system is still present in our day.

Second, the tollgate provides a metaphor not just for the behavior of Ananias and Sapphira but also for the decline of moral values in American culture. The tollgate episode typifies this attitude of "anything goes, so long as you don't get caught." In effect, the tollgate becomes a symbol of all kinds of cheating. It represents parking-lot violations, of course, but also those more serious breaches of personal integrity and honesty that are rampant in our society. The cited statistics about lawlessness in America, along with the instances of corporate illegalities, support this general assertion. But long after the statistics fade in the memory, the tollgate will be remembered. It is an image which can become fixed in the mind and thus convey a whole complex of associations. Some possible connotations from the tollgate metaphor: the dishonesty of the driver of the little red Volkswagen, the dishonesty of Ananias and Sapphira, the dishonesty of our society in general, and maybe even our own temptations to fudge the truth and try to beat the system.

Finally, the tollgate metaphor is used in a striking reversal at the end of the sermon. In the conclusion, the tollgate is used to connote a different kind of scandal—the scandal of the cross. Here the symbol of sin becomes representative of redemption. Through its association with Calvary, the tollgate metaphor is utterly transformed into a great good. This transformation is made explicit with the words: "The tollgate to life, and life eternal, is a cross. And in a way that we will never fully understand, God has already paid the toll and set us free."

This is the resolution—not simply a return to the situation at the beginning of the sermon but a movement beyond the beginning to something better. The metaphor of the tollgate has become a controlling image which ties the entire sermon together, and which moves the sermon along toward a graceful end. Such is the power of story to provide images which endure, even after the details of the story are long forgotten.

8
Evaluating Effectiveness

In one of Von Schlegel's plays the curtain rises to show the inside of a theater where another audience is waiting for the curtain to rise. When it does, a second such scene is disclosed; then a third. By which time the original audience begins to grow uneasy and looks around to see if perhaps it too is on the stage.

—Paul Scherer[1]

Gauging Sermon Effectiveness

Did the sermon work? Was it effective? Did it achieve its desired purpose? Those are questions which are difficult to answer. Probably the least reliable method of gauging effectiveness is going by what people say at the back door when they shake the preacher's hand on the way out. Some of their responses are purposely ambiguous, like, "That was sure some sermon today, pastor". Others are downright lies, told in the name of common courtesy. Many compliments are no doubt sincere, but who knows how deeply they are felt? Still, we need some means of evaluating how we are doing.

For most people, sermons are a matter of personal taste. Add other variables, like the personality of the preacher and the context of the worship service, and evaluating preaching effectiveness is even more complicated. Nevertheless, if preaching is to be improved (and that should be the goal of every preacher), it is necessary to establish some guidelines for gauging homiletical results. To measure sermon effectiveness, it is vital to understand what sermons are supposed to do. Then maybe we can decide if they really did their job.

Criteria for Evaluating Sermons

"The ultimate goal in preaching," James Earl Massey said, "is to connect the hearer with the grace of God."[2] That is a lofty, audacious ideal. Yet, by the grace of God, sermons can do exactly that. Probably very few people remember the particulars of any given sermon for very long. But the impact of a given sermon can last a lifetime. Hence, the primary goal of a sermon is not to convey information, although that is usually involved. The primary goal is not to fill the memory with ideas, though that may happen, too. Rather, the primary goal of preaching is to help create an experience. Herbert H. Farmer said, "A sermon should have something of the quality of a knock on the door."[3]

A sermon should be an invitation to enter another world, to entertain another possibility, to experience another dimension to life. The goal of the sermon is not just to tell people the truth, "but to help them feel it brushing against the inside walls of their hearts."[4] It's not enough for people to hear about forgiveness; they must feel forgiven. It's not enough for people to know the right thing to do; they must be motivated to go out and do the right thing. This is what is meant when we describe the sermon as language event. Something is said, and something happens. That is the ultimate test for any sermon.

Criteria for Evaluating Stories

Like the larger sermon itself, stories within the sermon must be an invitation to enter another realm of perceiving reality. If people hear a story and are not able to envision a theme or subplot to the seemingly random events of life, the story has not done its work. The purpose of story is to establish an order to life and the possibility for parallels. If something happened once, even in a story, it might happen again.

In Christian preaching, there is another criterion for evaluating stories. Examples and illustrations in sermons must help the congregation to identify with the biblical story. This is what distinguishes the preacher as storyteller from all other tellers of tales. The preacher is consciously limited by the Story from the Bible. Hence, the meaning, message, or theme of any story used in a sermon must be in harmony with the biblical understanding of reality. When the remythologizing has been done, the new story must convey the same truth as that original biblical story which was demythologized. Thus, the original scriptural story is not denuded of its truthfulness or mystery but is interpreted and deepend by the nonscriptural stories which the preacher tells in the sermon.

Of course, the effect of specific stories may be highly personalistic. Some stories may resonate with the life experience of one listener and fail to elicit any response in another. The most any preacher can do is deal in probabilities. Through our knowledge of the people, we can select or create stories which have the potential of calling forth parallels in the experiences of the listeners. Hence, audience analysis and a thorough exegesis of the text must be amalgamated to produce that creative combustion necessary for revelatory stories to appear. Without question, this process is more art than science, more mystery than mastery, dependent as it is upon that ineffable imaginative spark which comes from Above. Still, if inspiration did not stop with the original autographs of Scripture and the Spirit is yet active in our world, then we can dare to believe that such stories can be given, even to us.

One Evaluation Method: The Sermon Feedback Group

One possible way to judge preaching is through the use of a sermon feedback group. It requires some degree of courage and honesty, both on the part of the preacher and on the part of the group members. Nevertheless, it is one means of assessing what kind of impact a sermon or a series of sermons achieves. I have done this twice, once shortly after I came to the church as pastor with the Pastor Search Committee serving as the feedback group. The second time, I selected a group of perceptive laypersons from among the congregation, seeking to assemble a representative group of sermon listeners. I met with each group for three consecutive weeks to evaluate the Sunday morning messages. Each individual was asked to be present for the sermons on those Sundays and to fill out a sermon-response sheet prior to coming to the session.

Because the sessions were held on Sunday evenings, the sermons were fresh in the group members' minds. Still, it was interesting to learn what they remembered. I was surprised, and humbled, by how much they could recall. No doubt, knowing that they would be asked about the sermons provided some incentive to pay close attention. But I am convinced that most of those persons pay close attention anyway, even though when they will not be quizzed about what they heard. Of course, there are some .n every church who enjoy a regular Sunday morning snooze during the sermon. Increasingly, however, people come to worship because they want to, not merely out of habit or obligation. Those people listen to sermons attentively, carefully, and thoughtfully.

At first, it is excruciating to submit a much toiled-over sermon to the scrutiny of a bunch of laypersons who have no idea how much effort that sermon took to produce. Add to that the personal emotional investment in the sermon and there is potential for much wailing and gnashing of teeth when the sermon is criticized. Yet there is also something very affirming about hearing people relate what the sermon meant to them. After a level of trust was established, I discovered that I no longer dreaded the feedback sessions; in fact, I actually looked forward to them.

Something surprising happened when the feedback groups were disbanded. I immediately experienced a withdrawal reaction. I had developed a kind of "feedback dependency," and when the group process was over, it was hard to adjust. There was a vacuum of response. I no longer had a mechanism for dialogue. Did subsequent sermons hit their mark? Were my ideas communicated clearly? Did the themes and stories relate to their experiences? Was the Scripture made relevant? Without that weekly response forum, it was difficult to know. What's the lesson? When in doubt about preaching effectiveness, ask the people. A sermon feedback group can help you to know.

Learning from Storytelling

It was Willa Cather who said, "There are only two or three human stories, and they go on repeating themselves as fiercely as if they had never happened before."[5] Stories do tap into that universal reservoir of human experience because there is a fundamental connectedness to life. Stories connect us to one another and to God because ultimately all of our individual stories are but episodes in one comprehensive Story. Because of that relationship, much can be learned from storytelling. That applies not only to those who hear stories but also to those who tell them.

There is something about our devotion to God which drives us to recount that experience in narrative. The same Spirit which motivated the tellers and writers of oral traditions to produce the Bible is still at work. Even today, persons are sensitive to God's movement in human life, and when that sensitivity is translated into words, a story is born. We who dare to listen to, search for, and yes, create, stories discover that inspiration is still possible. Storytelling is a reaffirmation of faith, a belief in an ultimate mind and purpose, and an acknowledgement of the continuity which ties all stories finally together. In short, the storyteller can learn through the telling of tales about his own preconscious perceptions of the truth. He can learn about those fundamental beliefs that he has staked his life upon, whether he realized it or not. Thus, storytelling can open up new vistas of understanding for the storyteller as well as for those who hear the stories. Storytelling may, in fact, become a journey toward new theological horizons, a journey made not merely with the intellect but also with the affections and the will.

More Than We Mean to Tell

An important lesson from storytelling is the realization that stories, like all art, say more than we know we are saying. Mary McCarthy observed, "In any work that is truly creative, the writer cannot be omniscient in advance about the effects he proposes to produce."[6] In other words, we tell more than we mean to tell.

I find that conclusion confirmed time and again by informal feedback from persons who have heard my sermons. Repeatedly during conversations after preaching, I have been amazed that people heard in my sermons far more than I had intended to say. They had made their own connections through the stories, connections with events in their individual lives of which I was not even aware. More than once, people would claim to be quoting me word for word when in fact they were articulating their own unique applications of what they had heard the sermon say to them. Such is the inductive power of narrative, that through the particularities of focused incident a more general story emerges which is everyone's story. Ian Pitt-Watson expressed it like this: "When God speaks through the preacher, what is said is never adequate to express what is meant. But what is heard is often more than what is said."[7] So the Spirit works, through the teller and in the listener, to communicate that which is needful, that which is truthful, that which is deeper than words.

Images that Persevere

Not only do stories allow listeners to make personal connections, stories provide metaphors and images which invade the citadels of consciousness. As a result of one sermon that I preached at my church, for at least a few people the word *skateboard* refers to more than a platform with wheels. Through the story about the skateboards, some individuals were able to grasp a new understanding of the freedom and risks of human existence. Skateboards became for them a metaphor for the peril and the exhilaration inherent in life.

Instead of telling the story of the skateboards, I could have simply told the congregation that it is the risks in life which make possible the challenges and opportunities.

But I suspect that apart from the story, that kind of discursive statement would have made little impression. Trying to explain the theodicy question through philosophical argument is not very satisfying for most people. But metaphors from stories, however commonplace, can find their way into us where no philosophical argument can ever reach. Craddock said:

> The galleries of the mind are filled with images that have been hung there casually or deliberately by parents, writers, artists, teachers, speakers, and combinations of many forces. Images are replaced not by concepts but by other images, and that quite slowly. Long after a man's head has consented to the preacher's idea, the old images may still hang in the heart. But not until that image is replaced is he really a changed man.[8]

Invariably, it is the stories, or the images, that are hung in the heart and remembered: a skateboard, the doubting disciples on the mountaintop, a pastor in the Scottish highlands who wrote a hymn, a woman and a dog watching a movie, a man in a red Volkswagen who slipped under the tollgate, or a bug zapper in the backyard. Simple stories, biblical stories, historical stories, funny stories, all with one thing in common—they provided pregnant images which gave birth to memory. Images are integral to behavior, and those images have a life and vibrancy of their own. When set loose in the service of God through the sermon, stories can persevere in the heart until the work of grace is done.

Notes

1. Paul Scherer, *The Word God Sent* (New York: Harper & Row, Publishers, 1965), p. 81.

2. James Earl Massey, *Designing the Sermon: Order and Movement in Preaching* (Nashville: Abingdon, 1980), p. 18.

3. Herbert H. Farmer, *Servant of the Word* (Philadelphia: Fortress Press, 1964), p. 44.

4. Thomas H. Troeger, "Shaping Sermons by the Encounter of Text with Preacher," *Preaching Biblically*, ed. Don M. Wardlaw (Philadelphia: The Westminster Press, 1983), p. 172.

5. Belden C. Lane, *Storytelling: The Enchantment of Theology* (St. Louis: Bethany Press, 1981), Tape 1.

6. Mary McCarthy, "Settling the Colonel's Hash," *Literary Symbolism*, ed. Maurice Beebe (Belmont, Calif.: Wadsworth Publishing Company, Inc., 1960), p. 53.

7. Ian Pitt-Watson, *Preaching: A Kind of Folly* (Philadelphia: The Westminster Press, 1976), p. 21.

8. Fred B. Craddock, *As One Without Authority*, Third ed. (Nashville: Abingdon Press, 1979), p. 78.

9
Questions Nobody Asked

In Calvin's Geneva there lived a citizen who could well be the patron saint of countless lay people throughout the history of the church. When the city elders demanded that this Monsieur Belard appear before them to tell why he refused to attend divine services and hear the Word of God, he replied that he was more than willing to hear the Word of God, but not those preachers!

—Deane Kemper[1]

In his later years, well into his eighties, Dr. George Buttrick taught a solitary preaching course one afternoon a week during the spring semester of each year at The Southern Baptist Theological Seminary in Louisville, Kentucky. For two hours each Wednesday afternoon, we sat enthralled as one of the most prestigious preachers of our time sat before us and expounded his personal philosophy of preaching. It was the highlight of my seminary training. In order to vary his teaching technique beyond the lecture method, occasionally Dr. Buttrick would entertain questions from the class. He requested that we write down our questions on three-by-five-inch cards and hand them in at the beginning of the class period. Then, if time permitted and he deemed the questions fitting, he would answer selected queries at the end of the session.

Frequently I was amazed at the background and perception of my fellow class members. Some of the questions which Dr. Buttrick answered I did not know enough about to even ask. Some presupposed a level of homiletical study and knowledge which seemed far beyond the grasp of the average seminary student. One question, I recall, asked about a particular book written by Merrill R. Abbey. Now certainly Dr. Abbey was a distinguished preacher of a generation ago, but his name was hardly a household word for a group of master's-degree level seminary students. In fact, I had barely heard of Merrill R. Abbey before, much less read one of his books. Dr. Buttrick roundly commended Abbey's book in glowing terms and then, with a slight grin on his face, wryly admitted that he had planted that question himself. I came to discover that many of the questions which Dr. Buttrick had answered came from the same source. He had information he wanted to give us but instead of including it in his lectures, he packaged it under the guise of an answer to a supposed question.

I will declare my ruse from the outset. The answers, and the questions, in this chapter are mine. They are questions I would ask in response to a strong argument for storytelling in preaching. They are questions about why and how to tell stories in sermons. They are questions which I hope will provoke your own thinking about incorporating stories into your sermons.

1. How do you find good stories to use?
This is probably the most burning question, and the most difficult to answer. Good stories are exceedingly rare. They are precious treasures, pearls of great price. Some people will be disappointed in reading this book because it does not contain enough ready-made stories

which can be lifted out and used immediately. From what has gone before, it should be apparent that I do not advocate relying on books of sermon illustrations. Most of the stories are out of date, hackneyed, or not very good in the first place. I have spent literally hours looking for instant illustrations, only to be disappointed. In most cases, after a futile search for a touching story, I have either come up with one out of my own experience or not used one at all.

I asked a fellow pastor who engages in considerable storytelling in preaching what he does when he cannot think of a story to tell. "My people trust me," he said. "Sometimes the stories don't come, and my sermons are as dry as stones. But because they trust me, my people have learned to wait until the stories do come." Undoubtedly, there will be times when appropriate stories do not appear. At such times we fall back on all the other homiletical devices we can press into service and hope that somehow the Word of God will come through.

One significant factor in finding stories which are useful is to begin looking for the stories early in the sermon preparation process. I have found it to be very difficult to add stories later to a sermon outline, like adding water to condensed soup. If the stories do not emerge in the development of the sermon outline, they may not emerge at all. Hence, I look for stories at the beginning of my sermon research, or even before that. Occasionally, I will come across a good story and sit on it for weeks or even months before it can be used. Eventually, when such a story finds a complementary text, it is not unusual for an entire sermon to grow out of that union of story and Scripture.

In some respects, good stories are like manna from heaven. We are not likely to be able to hoard vast amounts of usable resources and pull them out at the drop of a hat. This is not to discount the value of a story file, although those which are exceedingly complex may be counterproductive. My file consists of a stack of loose clippings in a desk drawer. The problem is that our minds can only deal with so many items at the same time. Yet God has a way of providing what we need when we need it. Sometimes by engaging in other pastoral tasks and releasing our minds from a conscious search for sermon materials, we experience incidents and receive insights which do yield good stories.

More than once I have been stymied sitting at my desk laboring over a sermon, repeatedly letting the bucket down into the well of my memory and creativity and coming up dry. Then I disengage from sermon preparation to drive to the hospital to visit a sick church member. In the parking garage I witness a man who figured out a way to get by the tollgate and cheat the hospital out of the parking fee. Aha, a story! Or I go home and read in the newspaper about a dog who walked over eight-hundred miles from Colorado to Southern California to rejoin his former owners. Aha, another story! Somehow the stories do come. By intent or by accident, the stories appear. But we must be ever vigilant, ever receptive, ever ready to recognize them from whatever source they come.

2. What about stories from the Bible?

If the biblical narrative is strong enough, the text itself can function as the major story line of some sermons. Occasionally, it is possible simply to retell the biblical story and draw contemporary analogies and conclusions from it. I learned very early in my preaching career that it is generally easier to develop a sermon around a biblical incident than around a nonnarrative text. When a story is already built into the text, there are intrinsic opportunities for dramatic appeal and audience identification.

Hence, my advice to beginning preachers is to base sermons on story texts wherever possible. The Gospels are replete with parables and stories from the life of Jesus. The Book of Acts is a wonderful source of stories, as is much of the Old Testament. Use these built-in stories to gain confidence and develop style, then move on to the more didactic material of the New Testament Epistles or the Old Testament Wisdom Literature or the Pentateuchal paraenesis or the prophetic oracles.

There is another dimension to the stories of the Bible. Even paraenetic material may have a story behind it. The Epistles were written to specific church situations, and those contexts may provide underlying stories to be told. The dissension of the church in Corinth, for example, is a fascinating story of how the gospel message was interpreted and misinterpreted in a pagan society. Moreover, the story of the Corinthian church is integral to understanding Paul's letters to Corinth. Similarly, there is a story behind many of the Psalms or prophetic oracles. Thorough background study and exegetical research can identify the situations out of which much of this nonnarrative material was produced. Thus, diligent attention to commentaries and other reference works may yield not only a better comprehension of the meaning of the text, but also stories about the context which may be used in sermons.

3. How far should the story be pushed analogically?

It is not necessary to make every story an allegory, though some stories may provide several points of comparison. In fact, the search for point-by-point parallels may impose a strained interpretation on the story and strain the limits of credulity. At times one point of comparison may be enough. At other times, two or three analogies can be drawn from a single story. A few examples follow.

The major story of one sermon centered around the artificial heart program of a hospital in Louisville, Kentucky. By now, most people have heard of the Jarvik-7 mechanical heart and its principle advocate Dr. William DeVries. In telling the story of one of those sensational operations, I described a photograph which I had seen in a newsmagazine. The picture was taken in the operating room, and it showed two hearts sitting side by side: the old diseased heart which the surgeons had removed and the new mechanical heart which they were about to implant. From that image I drew two comparisons to advance the message of the sermon. First, Christ gives us a new heart when we receive Him in faith. Second, once we receive that new heart, there is no going back. I only made two analogies, though undoubtedly there could have been more. I resisted, for instance, the temptation to draw a parallel between the blood evident in the photograph and the blood of Christ. In my judgment, to have pushed the comparisons further would have unduly magnified the details of the story and breached the bounds of good taste.

Another sermon included a story about the Vietnam Memorial in the Constitution Gardens of Washington, DC. It has become one of the most visited sites in the nation's capital. I described a visit I had made there with my family and the reactions I observed in other visitors that day. The design of the Memorial is simple and breathtaking at the same time. Two black walls descend into the earth to form an angle, a *V*. On the walls are written the names of every American soldier who gave his life during the Vietnam War, over fifty-eight thousand of them. It's almost like a cemetery or mausoleum, except no bodies are buried there.

I noted as I recounted my visit to the Vietnam Memorial that the atmosphere around it is unlike any other tourist attraction in Washington. It seemed that everyone there was more than a casual sightseer. It was as if every visitor was there for a reason. Some scanned the walls to locate one name among the thousands—perhaps a son, husband, father, brother, cousin, or friend. Others stopped to read a whole panel of names. Some walked, as I did, from one end of the Memorial to the other and back again, taking it all in. All the while, there was very little talking, lots of snapshots, lots of quiet whispers, lots of silent meditation, but very little conversation. It was as if everyone had come to pay their respects to the dead. That's the way it was that Sunday morning after Jesus died. Three women made their way to a garden tomb to pay their respects to the dead.

That was the introduction to a sermon on the resurrection. I used a famous and meaningful landmark, the Vietnam Memorial, to create a mental and emotional image of the scene at Easter dawn. Thus, the entire setting of the contemporary story is used as analogy for the setting of the biblical story. Further, I remarked that while the women had come to mourn the dead, like the Vietnam Memorial, there was no body buried in that mourning place either. Thus, in an almost anachronistic way, we moved from our experience back to the experience of the first witnesses to the empty tomb. We transposed one frame of reference onto another, thereby making the biblical story contemporary to our own. It is not necessary to achieve a one-to-one correspondence between every aspect of the two stories. Enough connections have been made through these indicated similarities that the minds of the listeners can do the rest.

4. What about using stories for sermon introductions?

There are two schools of thought. My personal preference is to tell a story near the beginning of the sermon whenever appropriate. Since I customarily read the text upon which the sermon is based immediately before the sermon proper, the opening story serves several functions. First, it gains the immediate attention of the congregation, an attention which may have been dulled if the Scripture text is overly familiar. Second, telling a story as part of the sermon introduction momentarily diverts attention away from the Scripture text. Why would I want to do that? More than likely, many in the congregation have heard enough sermons and enough texts to think they know what the preacher is going to say about any given passage. By telling a story, especially a story which relates to the text in an indirect way, I allow the congregation to back away and then return to the text from a different direction. In the process, perhaps they will gain a new perspective on the text they had not seen before.

Finally, a story near the beginning may provide a melodic theme which can be heard later on or throughout the sermon. Either an opening scriptural story or secular story can be referred to again at certain salient points to provide continuity and movement in the sermon. Sometimes the conclusion can refer to the introduction to provide a sense of closure, although this device had best be used sparingly. Trying to tie the conclusion of every sermon to the introduction may become forced and will become so predictable that the sermon is deprived of any surprise element.

There are also arguments against the use of stories for sermon introductions. For one thing, it may not be necessary to introduce a sermon with an amusing anecdote or a heart-wrenching tale in order to gain the attention of the hearers. Many people have learned to direct their attention to the preacher simply because they know that it is the beginning of the sermon. In a questionnaire which I distributed to members of my congregation about my own preaching, I asked what I could do to get their attention at the beginning of the sermon. Several people responded that I already had it. The simple act of stepping into the pulpit and opening my Bible was enough to signal their attentiveness. Nothing else was required, for they were already with me at the outset.

A second objection to using stories as sermon introductions is more pungent. If the story is particularly memorable or moving, it may overwhelm the rest of the sermon. What follows may seem like a let-down if the sermon opens with a good story. Furthermore, the story may exert an undue influence on the rest of the sermon, so that the people cannot follow the progression of other ideas or images. Some stories are so provocative that they capture our imaginations and hold our minds hostage for a while. Such a story can be a powerful bully which dominates the sermon from that point on, whether intended or not. So you decide about using stories as sermon introductions. The fact that there are pluses and minuses to this approach may indicate the need for variety.

5. Must sermons be all deductive or all inductive in their use of stories?

Probably no sermon will fit the pattern perfectly. Indeed, the schematization of story usage into those two categories is admittedly artificial, but it does demonstrate the way stories can function. I searched long and hard to find for chapters 5 and 6 adequate examples of the two types of story usage. Most sermons do not fall so easily into either category but are a blend of deductive and inductive techniques. Further, most stories will be included with little conscious regard for precisely how they are being used. We learned to speak before we learned the rules of grammar. Similarly, we learned to tell stories before someone explained to us the rules of storytelling. Neither the rules of grammar nor those of storytelling were devised to stifle our ability to express ourselves. Rather, they are tools to help in refining our best instincts.

Storytelling in preaching is largely an instinctual matter, a matter far more artistic than scientific. Yet it is a skill which can be improved through study, practice, careful attention to technique, self-analysis, and feedback. In the end, there is no substitute for practical experience. Trying new sermon forms, experimenting with different story applications, and risking failure is the way to grow.

10
To Be Continued

On a Saturday afternoon in early fall I was domesticating, defining and privatizing my living space—constructing a redwood fence around my back yard. A man in his early thirties paused while walking his dog, watched me for a time, and asked if he could help. He explained that he loved to work with wood and had little to occupy his time. I accepted his offer, but before I could tell him when I would be working next he interrupted me: "There is something I must tell you now while I remember it. If I wait it may be too late. I don't know." He went on to explain that several years before he had been injured in an accident in which a small piece of metal had pierced the section of his brain which stores and controls memory. . . . Somehow he survived and the long road of rehabilitation began. He had learned to talk again with scarcely any impediment. But he still had no control over his memory. . . . Lacking a dependable memory he could not hold a job or plan for the future in spite of his technical intelligence being largely unimpaired. I listened to his story with a growing sense of tragedy. We planned to meet on the following Monday and work on the fence together but he never appeared.

—Sam Keen[1]

A Sense of Loss

My grandmother was a storyteller. Her father was a
country doctor in a little town in north central Texas
around the turn of the century, and her own childhood in
that environment brought back many sweet reminiscences. As a boy, I frequently would spend the night at my
grandmother's house, and just before bedtime she invariably would tell a story about her father and his adventures
as a man of mercy. He traveled all over the countryside
by horse-drawn buggy, delivering babies, taking medi-
cine to the sick, and doing those other doctoring tasks
which have become so institutionalized today.

I recall one episode when the weather was particularly
nasty—they call it a "norther" in Texas when a strong,
cold wind blows in from the north. My great-grandfather,
Dr. John Rice, had gone out that night to make an emer-
gency house call, traveling over dark dirt roads under an
overcast sky, with only the lanterns from the buggy to
light the way. He was on his way home around two o'clock
in the morning when somehow he became disoriented
and took a wrong turn. Suddenly the horse came to a stop
and would go no further. Neither shouts of encouragement nor the sting of the whip could move the beast. With
a wind-chill factor approaching zero and fatigue setting
in, Dr. Rice decided to remain in the carriage until dawn.
When the first light began to break, he understood why
the horse had stopped. Immediately before them lay an
ominous ravine. Both he and the horse surely would have
perished had not the animal held its ground.

What is the point to this episode? Any number of analogies could be drawn in the service of a sermon or personal
experience. All kinds of evocative metaphors are present:
traveling at night, following the horse, waiting until

dawn, and so on. For me the story has been memorable enough to provide different lessons at different junctures in my own life. But the point here is that stories are memorable, and memory is a precious prize. Without stories to tell, we are prisoners of the present moment, cut off from the past and held back from the future, unable to assess from whence we have come or to plan whither we are going. When sermons are robbed of their narrative force, it is as if a kind of spiritual amnesia is imposed upon the congregation. Without stories, memory is denuded of memories, and we do lose our way in the dark passages of our lives.

My grandmother told stories, dozens of stories, about a man I had never met and yet who was nonetheless a part of my past. I listened because they were entertaining but even more because I realized that they were a part of my heritage. As I grew older, I vowed that one day I would set my grandmother before a tape recorder and ask her to recreate those narratives that had nurtured my imagination and sense of identity. I never did. My grandmother is gone now with most of her generation, and those stories are but a fading memory. There will always be a sense of loss that I did not follow my best intentions and systematically record the details of those remarkable stories. Now, there are holes in my memory about where we came from and what our family was all about. My grandmother was the grand repository of our history, and through the stories she told she passed on the values which produced and were produced by that history. I regret that I cannot pass on that legacy in a more complete way to my own children because I did not pay close enough attention to the stories.

Still, the stories are not totally gone, for there are images from them which, even in subconscious ways, have helped to shape the person that I have become. Even in their fragments, the stories continue to exert a force. In his poem, "The Excursion," William Wordsworth wrote:

> . . . And, when the stream
> Which overflowed the soul was passed away,
> A consciousness remained that it had left,
> Deposited upon the silent shore
> Of memory, images and precious thoughts,
> That shall not die, and cannot be destroyed.[2]

I quoted that verse from Wordsworth at my grandmother's funeral because it expressed my deep convictions about the influence of her life on me. For over three decades she deposited upon the shore of my memory images and precious thoughts that shall not die and cannot be destroyed. You did not know her, but perhaps there have been persons in your life like that. Perhaps there have been persons who overflowed your soul like a life-giving stream: a parent, a spouse, a relative, a teacher, a coach, a neighbor, a pastor, a co-worker, a child, or a friend. Only you know who they are. Their passing is for you a silent anniversary of the heart. And yet, such precious ones are never lost. Even long after they are gone, a consciousness of them remains. We cannot call them back, but we can remember. We can remember their stories and find encouragement, direction, and new purpose for our own.

Conclusions About Storytelling in Preaching

Edmund Steimle, on a cassette recording, was asked to describe his hope for the future of the pulpit. His response so closely approximates the conclusion of this study that I quote it here.

What I would hope for when I go into any church and

listen to a sermon is that my story would be reflected in such a way, with such sensitivity and accuracy, that early on in the sermon I could say to the preacher, "Yeah, yeah, that's where I am; now let's go on together." In addition, I would like him to expose something of his story so that I know that this fellow is for real, and that he shares my doubts and my agonies, as well as my joys. And that with these two stories there would be, hopefully, an exciting, or at least intriguing, exposition of perhaps a familiar passage, so that I would see it in a way in which I hadn't quite seen it before in the light of my story and my situation.[3]

Thus, Steimle speaks of preaching as the merging of three stories: the story of the preacher, the stories of the listeners, and the Story from the Bible. When these stories are interwoven in the sermon, light can be shed on all three. In the process, something wonderful takes place. William Bausch said, "When many people are caught by, believe in, and celebrate the same story, you have a church."[4] So it is that the people of God have always discovered their common identity.

Preaching is difficult. Fosdick said, "Nothing can make preaching easy. At best it means drenching a congregation with one's lifeblood."[5] Even storytelling does not make preaching any easier. It may make preaching even more difficult. But it also makes preaching better. Of course, God can use any effort to accomplish His purposes, but why would we offer Him any less than our best? If stories do present the gospel in new and fresh ways, then why not use stories? If stories do help traverse from the biblical world view to our own, then why not use stories? If stories do narrow the distance between the pulpit and the pew, then why not use stories? If stories communicate with the rational and nonrational parts of our being, then why not use stories? If stories visualize the truth, then why not use stories?

"For we dream in narrative, daydream in narrative, remember, anticipate, hope, despair, believe, doubt, plan, revise, criticise, construct, gossip, learn, hate and love by narrative," said Barbara Hardy.[6] In order to live, we must use stories. In order to preach, we must use stories. In order to say anything about God and Christ and the church and what that has to do with anybody's life, we must use stories. Narrative is not an extraneous addition to preaching, but it is the lifeblood of sermons which are true to the Bible and true to people's lives.

Elie Wiesel tells a story in *The Gates of the Forest* which seems a fitting conclusion.

When the great Rabbi Israel Baal Shem-Tov saw misfortune threatening the Jews it was his custom to go into a certain part of the forest to meditate. There he would light a fire, say a special prayer, and the miracle would be accomplished and the misfortune averted. Later, when his disciple, the celebrated Magid of Mezritch, had occasion, for the same reason, to intercede with heaven, he would go to the same place in the forest and say: "Master of the Universe, listen! I do not know how to light the fire, but I am still able to say the prayer," and again the miracle would be accomplished. Still later, Rabbi Moshe-Leib of Sasov, in order to save his people once more, would go into the forest and say: "I do not know how to light the fire, I do not know the prayer, but I know the place and this must be sufficient." It was sufficient and the miracle was accomplished. Then it fell to Rabbi Israel of Rizhyn to overcome misfortune. Sitting in his armchair, his head in his hands, he spoke to God: "I am unable to light the fire and I do not know the prayer; I cannot even find the place in the forest. All I can do is to tell the story, and this must be sufficient." And it was sufficient.[7]

Gather the folk, break the bread, and tell the stories. Open the door for eucatastrophe to happen. Under God we can do no more; for God we must do no less.

Notes

1. Keen, *To a Dancing God* (New York: Harper & Row, 1970), pp. 25-26.

2. William Wordsworth, *A Wordsworth Anthology*, ed. Helen Davies (London: Collins, n.d.), p. 65.

3. Edmund A. Steimle, "Preaching as Story Telling," *Thesis Theological Cassettes*, 7 (Dec. 1976), No. 11.

4. William J. Bausch, *Storytelling: Faith and Imagination* (Mystic, Conn.: Twenty-third Publications, 1984), p. 197.

5. Harry Emerson Fosdick, "What is the Matter with Preaching?" *Harpers Magazine*, 157 (July 1928), p. 140.

6. Brian Wicker, *The Story-Shaped World* (South Bend, IN: University of Notre Dame Press, 1975), p. 47.

7. Elie Wiesel, *Gates of the Forest* (n.p., n.d.), p. 10.

Appendix 1:
Biblical Storytelling

Storytelling in the Old Testament

The Bible can help us learn how to tell stories. The preservation of much of the Old Testament over hundreds of years through oral transmission is instructive. Clearly, those ancient storytellers knew what they were doing. They fashioned their stories in such a way that they could be remembered and transmitted. Robert Alter has made some insightful studies into the artistry of the Old Testament storytellers. He noted, for instance, the significance of dialogue when narrative events seem especially important.[1] Narrators did not specify inner motivations or feelings. Rather, they allowed the characters to speak for themselves in order that we might draw our own conclusions about why the figures acted as they did.

Alter also maintained that an essential aim of the Hebrew authors was to provide a "certain indeterminacy of meaning, especially in regard to motive, moral character, and psychology."[2] This means that although the writers could have been more explicit, they purposefully withheld details in order to give their stories a sense of mystery and open-endedness. This economy of description forces the hearer/reader to use his own imagination and, more importantly, to posit his own interpretation of the story. Alter concluded, "Meaning, perhaps for the first time in narrative literature, was conceived as a process, requiring continual revision."[3]

Stories Jesus Told

Parable study in this century has focused to a large degree on the parables as literary entities. Except for the monumental work of Joachim Jeremias and the contributions of C. H. Dodd, parable study has taken a decisive literary bent since a new course was charted by Adolf Julicher. Many prominent scholars such as Ernst Fuchs, Eta Linnemann, Dan Via, John Dominic Crossan, Mary Ann Tolbert, Pheme Perkins, and Peter Rhea Jones have viewed the parables of Jesus primarily as "language events." Other more general New Testament students like Amos Wilder, Robert Funk, and Sally TeSelle share a similar perspective. Thus, there is a growing movement to treat the parables of Jesus not as dispensable stories which contain truth but rather as extended metaphors which are truth.

C. H. Dodd's classic definition of the parable is still valid.

[A] parable is a metaphor or simile drawn from nature or common life, arresting the hearer by its vividness or strangeness, and leaving the mind in sufficient doubt about its precise application to tease it into active thought.[4]

As many have noted, some form of comparison lies at the heart of any parable. Yet, it is often simplistic to try to reduce the parable to a single point. Mary Ann Tolbert wrote that "while the comparison element in the metaphor is most often expressed in a single image, the comparison element in the parable arises from the total

configuration of the story."[5] Hence, most modern interpreters of the parables of Jesus resist the temptation to
reduce their meaning to discursive statements. In short,
the parables mean more than mere propositions can express. It is the very nature of narrative to communicate
on different levels.

An important dimension of the power of Jesus' parables
is their ability to invite participation. As Pheme Perkins
observed, "Jesus does not finish the story. The hearer
must fill in what happens next."[6] The parables are not so
much gems of truth to be grasped as they are stories to be
entered into. Understanding is not possible so long as we
remain detached. But the magic of the parables is that we
are drawn into the dynamics of the story. That is why the
parables can "speak" to persons with different needs.
Within the story, each person has room to find his own
meaning. John Dominic Crossan said,

> It is one thing to communicate to others conclusions and
> admonitions based on one's own profound spiritual experi-
> ence. It is quite another thing to try and communicate that
> experience itself, or better, to assist people to find their
> own ultimate encounter. This is what Jesus' parables seek
> to do.[7]

Hearing parables—even if they are read they must be
heard—involves entry into another world. In that world,
to paraphrase Crossan, we may find that the deep, accepted structures of our world are shattered, and we are made
vulnerable to God.[8]

Finally, notice something of Jesus' art in parable telling.
Participation and involvement did not happen by accident. Jesus was a master storyteller. Robert Funk has
identified some characteristics of the major parables

which draw the listeners into the tales. They are as follows:

> Words and expressions are used parsimiously;
> Descriptors and adjectives are kept to a bare minimum;
> Feelings and emotions are mentioned only where essential;
> Direct speech is preferred to third-person narration;
> Only the necessary persons appear;
> The plot is simple;
> The story line is divided into three parts: opening, development, and crisis-denouement;
> repetition, rhythm, and assonance endow the prose of the parables with certain poetic qualities.[9]

Perhaps one reason that so many of the parables of Jesus were remembered and recorded was that He was so good at telling them. Ordinary, everyday experience took on a depth of meaning not seen before. As oral events, the parables of Jesus came alive for their hearers, and they continue to live.

Notes

1. Robert Alter, *The Art of Biblical Narrative* (New York: Basic Books, Inc., Publishers, 1981), p. 182.

2. Ibid., p. 12.

3. Ibid.

4. C. H. Dodd, *The Parables of the Kingdom* (New York: Charles Scribner's Sons, 1961), p. 5.

5. Mary Ann Tolbert, *Perspectives on the Parables* (Philadelphia: Fortress Press, 1979), p. 43.

6. Pheme Perkins, *Hearing the Parables of Jesus* (New York: Paulist Press, 1981), p. 4.

7. John Dominic Crossan, *In Parables: The Challenge of the Historical Jesus* (New York: Harper & Row, Publishers, 1973), p. 52.

8. John Dominic Crossan, *The Dark Interval: Towards a Theology of Story* (Allen, Texas: Argus Communications, 1975), p. 122.

9. Robert W. Funk, *Parables and Presence: Forms of the New Testament Tradition* (Philadelphia: Fortress Press, 1982), p. 20, 26.

Appendix 2:
A Psychological Rationale
for Storytelling

The Split-Brain Theory

Why do stories appeal to the rational and nonrational parts of our being? One explanation may be found in the split-brain theory. Physiologists have long known that the human brain is divided into two hemispheres—a left and a right. They have also known for some time that each hemisphere generally controls the opposite side of the body. But Robert Ornstein and others have suggested that the two hemispheres actually account for two modes of consciousness.[1] Roughly stated, the left hemisphere is logical, analytic, and verbal while the right hemisphere is intuitive, imaginative, and perceptual. Ornstein noted that this physical differentiation may parallel the observations of Roger Bacon, in 1268, when he said that there are two modes of knowing, argument and experience.[2]

More recently, Richard Restak has refined the theories of Ornstein. Restak believes that the left hemisphere is specialized for symbolic, verbal representation while the right hemisphere deals with nonverbal representations that mirror reality more directly.[3] In other words, the right hemisphere functions more on the basis of pictures, images, and gestalt than on the basis of logical arguments and discursive reasoning. This activity of the right hemisphere may explain why stories are so important to human consciousness and decision making.

Since Western culture has tended to emphasize "left brain" activity, dreams, myths, imagination, and prayer have often been disparaged as immature or irrational. An appreciation for the functioning of one half of our brains may contribute to a different assessment of the nonrational. Heretofore, stories, music, art, and other products of the imagination have been seen as the "frosting" to life, rather than the main course. But Rollo May queried, "What if [they] are not frosting at all, but the fountainhead of human experience?"[4] That very possibility ennobles stories far beyond their depiction as mere fanciful escapes from reality. Stories may, in fact, be more accurate representations of reality than logical propositions. Since stories can appeal to both dimensions of human consciousness, stories may be a uniquely holistic form of expression.

Stories and Decision Making

Albert Camus wrote in his notebook that the great philosopher must be a writer of fiction, for people are moved not by naked opinion but by images.[5] Reason alone seldom motivates people to change their actions, attitudes, or ideas. Human behavior is largely determined by feelings. Similarly, faith is lodged not so much in the intellect as in a more intuitive part of our natures. According to William Muehl, "When we are called upon in particular situations to make decisions, we ordinarily do so on the basis of a weird mixture of memory, emotion, conditioned response, and fragments of wisdom."[6] Frank Dance applied this insight to communication theory. He wrote that usually persons do not change behavior simply because they are told to. Rather, they must be engaged in the decision to change their behavior.[7] Such engagement invariably involves emotional appeal.

Good stories do appeal to the emotions. As a result, stories address those nonrational perceptions of reality that all of us carry around inside us. Stories help to overcome the dichotomy between thought and feeling because they encounter the whole person at the level of personal experience, either vicariously or in remembrance. When people are reached at the "gut level" of their lives, some response is inevitable. This is why Henry Mitchell believed that the best persuasion is not argument but art.[8] Argument involves the mind, but art involves the affections and the will. Stories tap into that vast reservoir of meanings we live by. Stories evoke that "catch of the breath, that beat and lifting of the heart," which according to Frederick Buechner, "is the deepest intuition of truth that we have."[9]

Notes

1. Robert E. Ornstein, *The Psychology of Consciousness* (New York: Viking Press, 1972), pp. 51-53.

2. Robert E. Ornstein, ed., *The Nature of Human Consciousness* (San Francisco: W. H. Freeman, 1973), p. 63.

3. Richard Restak, *The Brain: The Last Frontier* (New York: Bantam Books, 1984), pp. 250-252.

4. Rollo May, *The Courage to Create* (New York: W. W. Norton & Company, Inc., 1975), p. 124.

5. John Killinger, *The Saving Image: Redemption in Contemporary Preaching* (Nashville: Tidings, 1974), p. 13.

6. William Muehl, *All the Damned Angels* (Philadelphia: Pilgrim Press, 1972), p. 17.

7. Frank Dance, "Communication Theory and Contemporary Preaching," *Preaching: A Journal of Homiletics*, 3 (Sept.-Oct. 1968), p. 31.

8. Henry H. Mitchell, *The Recovery of Preaching* (San Francisco: Harper & Row, Publishers, 1977), p. 32.

9. Frederick Buechner, *Telling the Truth: The Gospel as Tragedy, Comedy, & Fairy Tale* (San Francisco: Harper & Row, Publishers, 1977), p. 98.

Appendix 3:
Understanding Analogy
and Metaphor

Central to an understanding of the transactive power of story are the categories of analogy and metaphor. Both analogy and metaphor rely on some type of correspondence, some connection between things which are in other respects different. In describing metaphor, Aristotle wrote, it is "giving a thing a name that belongs to something else."[1] Robert Frost defined metaphor poetically: "Saying one thing and meaning another, saying one thing in terms of another, the pleasure of ulteriority."[2] Both analogy and metaphor place one frame of reference alongside another for the purpose of comparison. Both are crucial to the transference of meaning through story.

Analogy and metaphor function to transmit knowledge about the unfamiliar by means of that which is familiar. To learn new things, we must make connections with things we already know. Since God can never be known or described as an objective entity, we use metaphors and analogies to speak about God. By applying that which is known to that which is unknown, we learn something about that unknown. Stories, like parables, have often been described as extended metaphors. Metaphors juxtapose two frames of reference in order to create novel surprises and evoke fresh images. Likewise, the surprise or suspense element which is a part of every story produces a leap in understanding when the tension is resolved. Moreover, through story, we are imaginatively a part of that resolution.

James Cox drew an important distinction between analogy and metaphor. Cox argued that analogies involve an explicit comparison while with metaphors the comparison is more implicit.[3] An analogy may be simple, like a simile which makes only one point of comparison. For example, you might say that reading this book has been like slogging through a swamp. In other words, it has been slow going. Analogies can also be more complex. From that analogy, you might find other points of correspondence. Not only has it been slow going, but it has also been tiring, frustrating, sloppy, and maybe even a little dangerous.

With metaphors, the comparisons are more implied. Jesus used a striking metaphor to talk about God. He called God *Abba*—Father. In our day, we have grown so accustomed to thinking of God as Father that the image is no longer shocking. But in Jesus' day it was a startling comparison, ascribing tender, fatherly attributes to the Holy One. As with most metaphors, there is no single point of comparison but a panoply of meanings. To say that "God is our Father" is to evoke a whole range of feelings and understandings. Stories, like the parable of the prodigal son(s), can provide metaphors, like the waiting father, which communicate on levels where we live. The parable does not specify the precise ways that God is like a waiting father, but we know almost intuitively that He is. The metaphor of the waiting father deepens with each telling as we reflect upon our own life experiences. It is a powerful image whose connotations are never exhausted.

Notes

1. Peter Rhea Jones, *The Teaching of the Parables* (Nashville: Broadman Press, 1982), p. 29.

2. Robert Frost, from "The Constant Symbol," *Literary Symbolism*, ed. Maurice Beebe (Belmont, Calif.: Wadsworth Publishing Company, Inc., 1960), p. 16.

3. James W. Cox, *Preaching: A Comprehensive Approach to the Design and Delivery of Sermons* (San Francisco: Harper & Row, Publishers, 1985), pp. 211-213.

Bibliography

Selected Recent Works Related to Storytelling in Preaching

Introductions to Preaching

Achtemeier, Elizabeth. *Creative Preaching: Finding the Words.* Nashville: Abingdon, 1980.
Don't be misled by the title. When Achtemeier talks about "creative" preaching, she does not mean experimental or avant-garde. Rather, *creative* means the full engagement of our abilities and labors, the faithful stewardship of our potentialities toward creating worthy sermons. The trademarks of creative preaching —sound exegesis, convincing logic, pleasing style—are always valid. This short volume is concise, practical, experiential, and helpful. It is full of pithy bits of advice such as: mastering basic English, knowing your people, developing an outline, writing out the sermon in manuscript form, not allowing illustrations to overpower the sermon. A preacher can easily use this book to critique his own preaching style.

Cox, James W. *A Guide to Biblical Preaching.* Nashville: Abingdon, 1976.
Another concise, to-the-point introduction. Though

somewhat superceded by Cox's more comprehensive
later work (see below), this book pays particular attention to the anatomy of the sermon. Of special interest
are Cox's suggestions for what to do with a point or idea
in a sermon. He shows how to fill out the basic skeletal
structure of a sermon outline, how to drive home the
meaning of major movements in the sermon. Best of all,
the book can be read in a mere portion of the afternoon
—not a bad investment of time.

_____. *Preaching: A Comprehensive Approach to the De-
sign and Delivery of Sermons.* New York: Harper &
Row, Publishers, 1985.
James Cox has established himself as one of the most
prolific contributors to contemporary preaching literature. He has edited several outstanding volumes of sermons as well as the yearly (Doran's) Minister's Manual,
published by Harper & Row. His earlier introduction to
preaching, cited above, is still useful. Also note the book
of interpretation essays which he edited: *Biblical
Preaching.* Now Cox has written his most complete
preaching textbook. The word *comprehensive* in the
title does not mislead. Thoroughly documented, reflect-
ing an admirable breadth of modern scholarship, this is
one of the best introductions to preaching in print.

Craddock, Fred B. *Preaching.* Nashville: Abingdon, 1985.
Alongside James Cox, Fred Craddock stands as one of
the most influential authors of homiletical literature today. His books on inductive preaching have not been
surpassed. He continues to contribute to preaching
commentaries for the new common lectionary. Here he
has written a basic introduction to preaching aimed at
the preaching student but helpful for seasoned preach-

ers as well. Craddock treats biblical interpretation and sermonic style with equal seriousness. This book is already making a name for itself. I called eleven religious book stores in our area. None had it in stock but most have sold the book and currently have it on order. I have no doubt that it will be widely used as a standard preaching textbook for years to come.

Fant, Clyde. *Preaching for Today.* New York: Harper & Row, Publishers, 1975.
A lively, readable, sometimes humorous book with much solid homiletical content. Fant acknowledges that preaching has received its share of criticisms, sometimes justified, but he goes on to present a strong case for the vibrancy of the pulpit. He advocates an "incarnational" style of preaching which stresses the meeting point of Scripture, preacher, and people. Hence, he speaks of learning to "exegete both the Bible and the congregation." The book explains how the idiom of the first century can be translated into the idiom of today. Because Fant assumes that communication is neither automatic nor easy, he details the necessary steps involved in producing sermons which truly speak, and are heard.

Kemper, Deane A. *Effective Preaching.* Philadelphia: The Westminster Press, 1985.
This book answers the question: What do you do after you have exegeted the text? In other words, what must happen beyond studying the Scriptures to make the sermon come alive? To address that issue, Kemper devotes most of his attention to sermon organization and illustration. His treatment is by no means exhaustive, but it is a start. A beginning preacher could do

worse than to read this relatively short book and follow its suggestions.

Killinger, John. *Fundamentals of Preaching.* Philadelphia: Fortress Press, 1985.
Killinger brings a decisive literary bent to sermon preparation. This is not to suggest that his style lends more to writing than to public speaking. Sermons are, of course, oral media. Still, some of the same literary principles which underlie written materials can be applied to sermons. Hence, Killinger likens preaching to storytelling, or sermons to drama. The result is a fairly complete introduction to preaching from a literary perspective.

Biblical Exegesis for Preaching

Cox, James W., ed. *Biblical Preaching: An Expositor's Treasury.* Philadelphia: The Westminster Press, 1983.
A compendium of essays from an array of biblical scholars and preachers including Elizabeth Achtemeier, George Beasley-Murray, Reginald Fuller, Eric Rust, Edward Schweizer, Frank Stagg, Krister Stendahl, and more. Each essay discusses how to preach from a particular portion of Scripture. Thus, guidelines are presented for preaching from every part of the Bible, from the primeval narratives of Genesis to the eschatological texts of Revelation. The book includes an incredible amount of practical suggestions and sermon ideas. The over two-hundred hundred sermon outlines alone justify the cost of this "expositor's treasury."

Keck, Leander E. *The Bible in the Pulpit.* Nashville: Abingdon, 1978.
A carefully outlined book which identifies causes in the

malaise of biblical preaching and provides suggestions for its renewal. The major contribution of this book is Keck's redefinition of biblical preaching. He bids farewell to moralizing and proposes an interpretative process based on the Scriptures themselves. Keck concludes the book with three of his own sermons to demonstrate how those principles may be applied.

Rohrbaugh, Richard L. *The Biblical Interpreter: An Agrarian Bible in an Industrial Age.* Philadelphia: Fortress Press, 1978.
Rohrbaugh acknowledges the difficulty of interpreting an agrarian Bible in an industrial age. Because the setting of the Bible was so different from our own, an understanding of the context can help us better to understand the text. Rohrbaugh assumes that there is a "consanguinity of experience" between the biblical writers and modern interpreters, but it is often masked by cultural trappings. It is the task of hermeneutics to translate this experience into a different social setting. The result is a stimulating little book which pictures the preacher as a vital link in the intrepretive chain.

Thompson, William D. *Preaching Biblically: Exegesis and Interpretation.* Nashville: Abingdon, 1981.
One of the clearest statements about biblical exegesis and interpretation available. Thompson draws a crucial distinction between exegesis and hermeneutics. Both exegesis—understanding what the text meant to those who first read it—and hermeneutics—understanding what the text means today—are vital to preaching. Thompson demonstrates how both of these movements contributes to the interpretation of Scripture. This book is important, fundamental, must reading.

333

Sermon Organization and Delivery

Bartow, Charles L. *The Preaching Moment: A Guide to Sermon Delivery.* Nashville: Abingdon, 1980.
One of the better volumes on the "how to" of sermon delivery. Bartow places emphasis on the sermon not as presentation but as personal event. Yet attention to diction, enunciation, and "kinesic behavior" (movement) cannot be ignored. The preaching moment must evidence spontaneity and preparation. This small volume can help to make that happen.

Chartier, Myron R. *Preaching as Communication.* Nashville: Abingdon, 1981.
Another in the "Abingdon Preacher's Library" series, this book draws upon modern communication theory to enhance preaching. Chartier investigates the process of communication in order to identify implications for preaching. Some of his conclusions: simplify ideas, repeat key concepts, organize into successive stages, and relate new ideas to old ones. In addition, he discusses aspects of nonverbal communication. These principles can facilitate virtually any kind of communication, whether from the pulpit or between individuals. Even if it doesn't help your preaching, it might help your relationships.

Fasol, Al. *A Guide to Self-Improvement in Sermon Delivery.* Grand Rapids: Baker Book House, 1983.
Another practical book concerned with the vocal and physical delivery of the sermon. Fasol's premise is that the goal of sermon delivery is to "maximize the message and minimize the messenger." Attention is given to improving articulation, vocal tone, pacing, and ges-

tures. The book includes several self-evaluation exercises in the appendices.

Hoefler, Richard Carl. *Creative Preaching and Oral Writing*. Lima, Ohio: C.S.S. Publishing Company, 1978.
Comparing the sermon to a bumblebee, Hoefler notes five basic parts: head, body, stinger, legs, and wings. From this analogy, he proceeds to describe how the sermon can be written for oral presentation. Though not for everyone, his technique of "manuscript preaching" may be a perfect solution for some preachers. And even those who use a different method may get a few ideas from his ingenious style. An interesting book from from a lesser-known publishing company.

Massey, James Earl. *Designing the Sermon: Order and Movement in Preaching*. Nashville: Abingdon, 1980.
This is a book about sermon organization. Massey argues that there is not one way to organize a sermon, but many. To illustrate, he analyzes the design of three types of sermons: the narrative/story sermon, the textual/expository sermon, and the doctrinal/topical sermon. He concludes the book with an example of each type. By focusing on order and movement, sermon design becomes an important ingredient in effective preaching.

Nichols, J. Randall. *Building the Word: The Dynamics of Communication and Preaching*. San Francisco: Harper & Row, Publishers, 1980.
Nichols does not write, prepare, or create sermons. He "builds" them. Ideas and language are his specs and materials. Following this novel approach, he uses insights from communications theory, pastoral psychology, and Christian education. In the process, he

challenges much conventional wisdom about preaching. For example, he questions whether the purpose of the sermon introduction is to get people's attention. After all, Nichols asks, "When was the last time anyone saw a preacher step into the pulpit at sermon time and not have everyone's attention?" Such is the thrust of this insightful, stimulating perspective. Although it is advertised for beginning preachers, I can envision how more experienced preachers might read this book, find their cherished shibboleths challenged, and their preaching renewed.

Young, Robert D. *Be Brief About It.* Philadelphia: The Westminster Press, 1980.
At last, a convincing argument for brevity in the pulpit! This book attacks the notion that more is more. Young claims that good planning can shorten sermons and heighten their impact. His book supplies guidelines for briefer sermons, and some samples to show what those kind of sermons look like. Even if these observations don't make our sermons shorter, they very well could make them better.

Narrative Preaching

Bass, George M. *The Song and the Story.* Lima, Ohio: C.S.S. Publishing Company, 1984.
Another offering from the C.S.S. publishing house. Perhaps not available in many retail outlets, but it is worth the search. Bass draws explicit connections between storytelling and preaching. He admits there are certain problems inherent in story preaching such as the way meaning is conveyed indirectly. Nevertheless, he argues for a sermonic form which utilizes many of the characteristics of story.

Brown, David M. *Dramatic Narrative in Preaching.* Valley Forge: Judson Press, 1981.
The primary focus of this book is the use of first-person narrative in preaching or the dramatic monologue sermon. Others, such as Alton McEachern, have written on this specialized use of story. The value of Brown's book goes beyond that narrow application in a dramatic monologue. Brown provides helpful criteria which can be used to fashion any type of narrative, not just dramatic monologues. Hence, this book is recommended for that broader purpose. If you are particularly interested in the first-person narrative, I would recommend McEachern's book *Dramatic Monologue Preaching,* published by Broadman Press.

Jensen, Richard A. *Telling the Story.* Minneapolis: Augsburg Publishing House, 1980.
This is one of the finer books on narrative preaching. Jensen demonstrates the weaknesses of didactic preaching in order to provide a rationale for story preaching. He tells three story sermons to allow the mode itself to convey its power. If you are only going to read two or three books on narrative preaching, let this be one of them.

Lowry, Eugene L. *Doing Time in the Pulpit.* Nashville: Abingdon, 1985.
This follow-up to his previous work: *The Homiletical Plot,* is Eugene Lowry's latest contribution to the field of narrative preaching. Lowry conceives of the sermon as "an ordered form of moving time." Thus, there is an intimate relationship between narrative and preaching. In the book Lowry shows how the time of the story and that of the sermon can become one and the same. An

inventive and intriguing approach, this perspective
defies explanations. Read it and see for yourself.

_____. *The Homiletical Plot: The Sermon as Narrative
Art Form*. Atlanta: John Knox Press, 1980.
The companion volume to *Doing Time in the Pulpit*,
this is Lowry's seminal work in narrative preaching. He
approaches the sermon as an author would approach a
story, with a concern for plot development and resolution. With this understanding, the sermon is a narrative
art form, a sacred story to be told. Just as the plot of a
story moves through certain stages, so the movement of
a sermon occurs along story lines. Equilibrium is upset,
ambiguities are heightened, climax and denouement
follow. This is a most original and provocative means of
sermon composition.

Mitchell, Henry H. *The Recovery of Preaching*. San Francisco: Harper & Row, Publishers, 1977.
Mitchell draws upon the narrative tradition of much
black preaching to reclaim the original story element of
biblical preaching. Part of the book is an edited version
of the author's 1974 Lyman Beecher Lectures on
Preaching at the Yale University Divinity School. The
book is an eloquent apology for the power of stories to
move persons "transconsciously" toward deeper spiritual maturity. Its insights are applicable, not just to
black preaching but to all preaching which endeavors
to reach persons at the deep level of commitment and
will.

Steimle, Edmund A., Niedenthal, Morris J., and Rich,
Charles L. *Preaching the Story*. Philadelphia: Fortress
Press, 1980.
Put this one near the top of your list of books on narra-

tive preaching. The book is actually a collection of essays organized around the storytelling theme. The authors present important statements on the theory of narrative preaching, along with representative sermons from such preachers as Joseph Sittler, Frederick Buechner, and Edmund Steimle. Also included are essays from a number of guest contributors. After reading this book, it is hard not to be convinced of the value of narrative preaching.

Troeger, Thomas H. *Creating Fresh Images for Preaching*. Valley Forge: Judson Press, 1982.
An intriguing look into the psychology of sermon development and the religious imagination. Interspersed with sermon fragments, suggestive reflections, unfinished ideas. Difficult to categorize. Some portions are almost stream of consciousness, full of images, insights, inspiration.

Wardlaw, Don M., ed. *Preaching Biblically: Creating Sermons in the Shape of Scripture*. Philadelphia: The Westminster Press, 1983.
One of the most helpful explanations of narrative preaching. Each contributor comments on his method, makes exegetical observations about the text, and then provides the resultant narrative sermon. Here we are able to follow homiletical theory all the way through practical application. Perhaps an overstatement of the value of narrative preaching is presented, but it is nonetheless convincing. Extremely well done.

Waznak, Robert. *Sunday after Sunday: Preaching the Homily as Story*. New York: Paulist Press, 1983.
A Roman Catholic viewpoint on narrative preaching. He integrates the story of the preacher, the story of

God, and the story of the listener into a narrative treatment of the homily. Although the book is specifically aimed at a Roman Catholic readership, with numerous references to various encyclicals and other in-house documents, the book is conversant with Protestant traditions and contains many useful insights. Both priests and ministers would be well served by reading it.

Storytelling

Baker, Augusta and Ellin Greene. *Storytelling: Art and Technique.* New York: R. R. Bowker Company, 1977.
An excellent treatment of the mechanics of storytelling. It is a primary reference work used by many public librarians and other storytelling professionals. The bibliography contains a wealth of possible sources for stories, as well as other definitive works in the storytelling literature. This book was recommended to me by a librarian who specializes in storytelling. Although the orientation is more toward secular stories, the principles of storytelling work equally well with sacred stories. There are many other books on storytelling, some classics, but I believe this one is the best.

Bausch, William J. *Storytelling: Faith and Imagination.* Mystic, Conn.: Twenty-third Publications, 1984.
An outstanding book on storytelling from a religious perspective. Bausch includes a number of stories throughout the text to drive home the importance of story to religious expression. The book is both a wealth of stories and a beautiful philosophical statement about the storytelling process. An unusual blending of narrative theology and actual stories. Highly recommended.

Confessional Preaching

Buechner, Frederick. *Telling the Truth: The Gospel as Tragedy, Comedy & Fairy Tale*. San Francisco: Harper & Row, Publishers, 1977.
A book about sermonic technique from a master story-teller. Buechner is both a successful novelist and an ordained minister. Although he has written subsequent books which are even more autobiographical, this work contains in its most complete form the Buechner theology of preaching. Somehow the truth of the preacher's own life must come through the sermon. Beuchner shows how the personal faith journey can be shared as a corporate experience.

Claypool, John R. *The Preaching Event.* Waco: Word Books, 1980.
The 1979 Lyman Beecher Lectures on Preaching. This is perhaps the definitive book on confessional preaching. Claypool explains how self-giving is at the root of both authentic preaching and authentic Christian living. By making available our own vulnerability and woundedness to the people to whom we preach, we offer the possibility of true healing.

Inductive Preaching

Craddock, Fred B. *As One Without Authority*. 3rd ed. Nashville: Abingdon, 1979.
Once upon a time preachers spoke with authority: the authority of the office of clergyman, the authority of the church, and the authority of the Scripture. Most sermons could take the form of pronouncements—*Thus saith the Lord*. Today, for sermons to even get a hearing, a more indirect approach is needed. That is where

inductive preaching comes in. In this first of Craddock's books on the inductive method, he explains how induction works. My own copy of this book is from the second printing of the third edition. That gives a clue about its enduring value.

———. *Overhearing the Gospel.* Nashville: Abingdon, 1978.
In many respects a companion volume to *As One Without Authority.* Craddock uses the example of Soren Kierkegaard to illustrate how the gospel can be overheard in an indirect way. Under this method, story becomes a primary vehicle of the sermonic message. The book is an outgrowth of the 1978 Lyman Beecher Lecture series.

Lewis, Ralph L. and Gregg Lewis. *Inductive Preaching.* Westchester, Ill.: Crossway Books, 1983.
Perhaps the most complete exposition of the inductive method. The authors present step-by-step instructions for creating inductive sermons, as well as two examples. They recognize the value of storytelling to draw listeners into the movement of the sermon. The book is repleat with helpful graphics which visually demonstrate how stories can be incorporated into the inductive process. Appendices include a checklist of inductive characteristics, and a catalogue of notable inductive preachers from Christian history.

Parables as Language Events

Crossan, John Dominic. *The Dark Interval: Towards a Theology of Story.* Allen, Texas: Argus Communications, 1975.
A study into the subversive quality of parables. Crossan

maintains that the parables of Jesus actually subvert our common values and worldview with a whole new picture of reality. The book suggests a radical reinterpretation of the function of parables. As such, it is provocative, maybe even controversial. This is not a commentary on the individual parables, but a book to expand the horizons of how we view the parables in general.

————. *In Parables: The Challenge of the Historical Jesus.* New York: Harper & Row, Publishers, 1973.
A literary approach to the parables of Jesus. Crossan values the parables for their ability to invite participation. They draw the hearer into the tale, and in following the movement of the story, the listeners experience the truth of the parable in the hearing. He cites a number of specific parables to show how this participatory process happens. Not a particularly easy book, but fresh, original, unique.

Jeremias, Joachim. *The Parables of Jesus.* 2nd rev. ed. New York: Charles Scriber's Sons, 1972.
In some respects, this volume in miscast in this category. Jeremias' approach to the parables is more historical than literary. Nevertheless, this is a book of such monumental significance that it must be included in any bibliography of recent parables studies. Jeremias pays particular attention to the way the parables were adapted by the early church. Although the manner of organization makes it difficult to use this book as a commentary on individual parables, it is still invaluable in providing an understanding for how the parables may be actualized.

Jones, Peter Rhea. *The Teaching of the Parables.* Nashville: Broadman Press, 1982.
If you want one book which reflects the conclusions of major modern parable studies, this is it. The first chapter is an overview of recent trends in parable research, and the second chapter explores the nature of the parable. Chapter Three reflects the literary concerns which inform Jones' approach, while the remainder of the book is basically a commentary on the individual parables. This is a book of unusual quality, presented in a readable style.

Perkins, Pheme. *Hearing the Parables of Jesus.* New York: Paulist Press, 1981.
A book which is both popularly written and academically sound. Perkins conducts a literary analysis of each parable, along with historical background, to determine what the parable is saying. She proceeds to raise questions about the human and religious significance, so that the hearer must ask, "How do I respond to this story?" In addition, there are study questions at the end of each chapter. This book could be used with confidence for individual study, or as part of an adult study group program.

TeSelle, Sallie McFague. *Speaking in Parables.* Philadelphia: Fortress Press, 1975.
Not so much a book about the parables as it is a book about the theology of storytelling. TeSelle examines the functioning of metaphor in parable, poem, and story. She concludes that "the story as extended metaphor is the key form of the New Testament." Hence, she reclaims narrative as intrinsically important to religious expression.

Tolbert, Mary Ann. *Perspectives on the Parables*. Philadelphia: Fortress Press, 1979.
Tolbert describes the parables of Jesus as "polyvalent or plurisignificant." By that she means that they are open to multiple interpretations. Her book designates the parameters within which the parables can be faithfully interpreted. She offers guidelines for interpretation which take into account the possibility for different levels of meaning without sacrificing the essential message of the parables.

Via, Dan Otto, Jr. *The Parables: Their Literary and Existential Dimension*. Philadelphia: Fortress Press, 1967.
Although somewhat older than most of the books cited in the bibliography, this remains a pivotal work in parable study. Via bases his interpretations of the parables on their inherently dramatic form. He was a pioneer in applying categories of literary criticism to parable research. His way of viewing the parables—as essentially tragic or comic—provides a framework for making every parable contemporary.

Tape Recordings

Lane, Belden C. *Storytelling: The Enchantment of Theology*. 4 Tapes. St. Louis: Bethany Press, 1981.
A series of four tapes about storytelling in preaching. Tape 1: Five Characteristics of the Revelatory Tale. Tape 2: Stories of the Rabbis. Tape 3: Christian Storytellers—An Alternative Theological Tradition. Tape 4: The Telling and Loving of One's Own Stories. A valuable set of messages to be heard again and again.

Steimle, Edmund A. "Preaching as Story Telling." *Thesis Theological Cassettes*, 7 (December 1976), No. 11.

Contains Steimle's personal philosophy of preaching along with a Steimle sermon preached on location in a local church. Steimle traces the development of his interest in storytelling, as well as his hope for the pulpit of tomorrow.